The TRAINER'S DESK REFERENCE

Tips, Checklists & Summaries

Geoffrey Moss

KOGAN
PAGE

Previously published by Moss Associates Ltd, New Zealand, as *The Trainer's Handbook*.
This edition first published in Great Britain in 1991 by Kogan Page.

Kogan Page Limited
120 Pentonville Road
London N1 9JN

© Geoffrey Moss 1987, 1988, 1989, 1990, 1991

British Library Cataloguing in Publication Data

A CIP record for this book is available from the British Library.

ISBN 0 7494 0462 0

Typeset by Moss Associates Ltd
Printed and bound in Great Britain by
Clays Ltd, St Ives plc

JANE MCQUEEN
ROOM 105
HMC

Jane McDuee

The
TRAINER'S
DESK
REFERENCE

CONTENTS

PREFACE

Training has assumed an increasingly important role in organisations in all countries.

This book aims to explain the basic principles of training in simple terms — to take the jargon and the gobbledygook out of training. It is full of helpful checklists and ideas from trainers from many countries, giving it a universal relevance.

The book was written to help new trainers get started and to help managers understand, plan and evaluate training. Managers and supervisors must be involved. Without their commitment, support and encouragement the training will be wasted. They must also monitor training carefully to see how effective it is. How does it affect job performance and staff morale? And how much does it cost?

Good training will bring rewards if it is in line with organisational development policies. Initially, training should be targeted at key result areas — areas where new technology, new procedures or new policies have created change. Today nothing is really permanent except change.

The goal of training should be to achieve long-term improvement in the way staff do their jobs. The aim of training should be to inspire action rather than fill with knowledge.

This is a practical guide for all trainers, whether they are involved in full-time or only occasional training. It has been well field-tested and is sold in many countries. It was first published in New Zealand as *The Trainer's Handbook*, then by the Singapore Institute of Management for Asia and is a best seller in Australia.

I hope this edition for the United Kingdom will help trainers and managers plan interesting, challenging and enjoyable training sessions. People learn best when they are having fun — so use your imagination and enjoy your training.

GRM
April 1991

ACKNOWLEDGEMENTS

My grateful thanks to all my friends and colleagues from many countries who shared their ideas with me in training sessions, workshops and seminars over many years.

Special thanks to Joyce Moss as editor.

INTRODUCTION

I once worked on a dairy farm where a young lad was looking after the calves. It was his job to wean and to feed them — to take them away from their mothers and to teach them to drink out of a bucket.

One day I noticed he was having trouble with a certain calf. It had sucked his hair, it had sucked his ear. In fact, it had done almost everything but drink out of the bucket. In utter desperation, after commenting on the animal's ancestry, the lad picked up the bucket of milk and poured it over the calf, saying: "Damn you, if you won't drink the milk, let it soak in!"

Often trainers do precisely the same sort of thing during a training session. In utter desperation (and because it's usually the easiest way) they lecture their audience, expecting their words to 'soak in'.

Most people are keen to compete and to master new skills. We have an instinct to be curious, to explore, to find out, and to understand. We can be stimulated by gimmicks and novelties. The thought of solving a problem or of completing a task can be a stimulus. A reward or the prospect of one can awaken in us the desire to learn. On the other hand, we become frustrated and lose interest when we believe the goal is unattainable or when we think the exercise is pointless. Try to make training challenging and fun, using a variety of techniques, with as much participation as possible.

1 THE LEARNING PROCESS

After you have read this chapter you should be able to:

List some important principles of learning

Make your training more effective when teaching adults

Learning is Personal

Learning is a very personal process—in terms of the learner's own needs and interests. It is an active process—not the 'pouring' in of a passively received message. The learner reacts to the message and the learning encompasses a change in behaviour, be it mental, emotional, or physical. It can also be stressful.

Conducive Conditions

Managers and trainers can do much to stimulate and encourage learning by selecting methods that will provide the experiences which promote learning. They should aim also for physical and psychological climates that will be conducive to learning.

Comfort Assists Learning

We learn best when we are comfortably at ease, without too many distractions.

A farmer will often prefer a field, a barn or a woolshed as a site for learning, provided it is physically comfortable. This physical comfort is much more important than most people realise. A 'schoolroom' situation is often not conducive to adult learning, especially if the memories of school-day learning are not particularly happy ones. Remember that most of the factors that inhibit learning are self imposed, by the learner.

Adapt teaching to needs

The 'psychological climate' can be manipulated in various ways. The teaching should be adapted to the needs and vocabularies of your audience — to the speed of their learning and to their previously acquired knowledge. Strive to give the members a feeling of being at ease. Make them feel they know something. Examine the individual differences of opinion and strive not to embarrass any of the members. Help them to see they can disagree without being disagreeable.

Some Important Principles of Learning

Involvement

We are more likely to remember a solution we have worked out for ourselves than one which has been thought out for us—also to act on the decisions we have made for ourselves rather than on those that have been made for us.

Readiness

Learning will take place more quickly if we want to learn and are ready to learn.

Reinforcement

Repetition and meaningful exercises in a non-hostile environment will overcome 'interference' from other learning.

Intensity

Intense, dramatic, or vivid experiences are likely to make an impression by capturing the attention and strengthening the impact.

Association

Learning that is related to our own experiences (so that similarities and differences can be seen) is more likely to be remembered.

Distribution

Learning that is distributed over several short lessons is more effective than if it is crammed into a single, long lesson.

Effectiveness

Learning is more likely to occur when it is satisfying than when it is embarrassing or annoying. Approval encourages learning.

Capacity

Most of us remain at a stage that is far below our real capacity for learning, working and achieving.

(Irri Adec is a mnemonic which will help you remember these principles)

Drawing on Combined Experiences

Often I have worked with groups whose totalled years of experience in the topic under discussion have added up to several hundreds. How can any tutor with, say, 25 years' experience hope to match the combined experience of such a group? Good tutors do not try to do so. Rather they seek to 'cash in' on other people's experiences and to tap this knowledge by leading a discussion along planned lines. Adults learn well when they are sharing experiences. Very often they will relate better to one another than to the professional, who frequently lacks practical experience in the topic.

The professional tutor, teacher, or extension worker has (or should have) the skills to define a problem; to decide on objectives; and to draw people out, so that they share their experiences and thus work toward a planned goal.

At the same time, the tutor needs to be firm enough to know when to interrupt people who digress or who start to monopolise a discussion. Like the good chairman, a good tutor needs to keep one eye on the clock, for time usually needs to be rationed.

Everybody has Commitments

Every day pressures at home can cause adults to 'turn off' for periods which break the concentration necessary for effective learning.

An adult's learning is interwoven with many other activities and responsibilities. Younger persons, with fewer responsibilities, usually have more time to concentrate on learning.

There are advantages in running a course in a residential centre, away from home and work environments. You take the members away from their daily responsibilities. If you can keep them fully occupied, with work and with social activities, you will see greater concentration given to your discussion topics.

New Tricks for Old Dogs

Research has dispelled the myth that an old dog cannot be taught new tricks.

Increasing age does affect one's performance speed and reaction time. The result? We absorb learning at a somewhat slower rate. This does not mean any lessening of the *ability* to learn. Many people, in all fields of creative endeavour, make their biggest contribution in later life.

But, because the learning *rate* for adults does tend to be slower, the lessons must be 'hammered home' by repetition, by examples and by demonstrations.

Our Declining Faculties

An adult's vision usually changes rapidly between 40 and 50 years of age. Hearing and physical reactions also decline. We are, however, often loath to acknowledge our physical failings and defects. The tutor needs to be aware of these difficulties and must ensure that everybody can hear and see adequately.

- Make sure your visual aids are really 'visible'.
- Check that the acoustics are adequate.
- Try to shut out any interfering noises.
- Encourage clear, distinct speech.

How We Learn

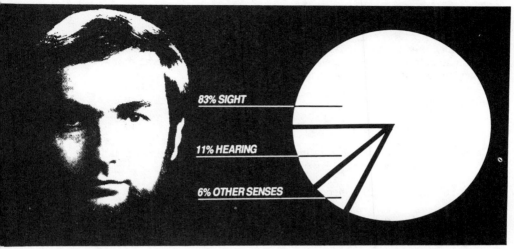

83% SIGHT

11% HEARING

6% OTHER SENSES

Figure 1

Adults Vary Enormously

'For you to teach John Latin, it is not enough just to know Latin—you must also "know" John'.

The tutor should always know as much as possible about the needs and the knowledge level of each of the students before planning any training programme.

Adults, like children, learn at varying speeds. There are thus advantages in having a variety of training tools in your bag of tricks. Each of them will suit some people better than others.

Variety in Methods

People of all ages learn more rapidly from a variety of teaching methods than from a single one.

In general, we learn best from actually doing a job, next best from what we see, then from what we read and hear. A 'lecture' is an ineffective way of teaching—but if it is used in conjunction with other techniques, its effectiveness can be increased. The spoken word should be reinforced with visual aids, demonstrations, and handouts.

Whenever possible, repetition in a non-threatening environment is a valuable way to learn a new skill.

A variety of teaching techniques is perhaps the best way to reinforce the learning process—but there is no one way that is best for everybody.

Involvement Aids Learning

From the setting of the goals and objectives to the final evaluation, every course member should be heavily involved.

Traditionally, the lecture has been the most common method of teaching. It is probably also the most ineffective. The tutor should in fact use as many techniques as possible to involve the students.

Some of these techniques are:

- Direct, purposeful experiences ('learn by doing')

- Contrived experiences ('mock-up' situations, play acting, models, demonstrations, exercises)

- Group and paired discussions

- Field trips and demonstrations

- Forums and panel discussions

- TV and films

We learn best when we are enjoying our learning—when we are being challenged and entertained by a variety of exercises and competitions.

Avoid Ridicule

The adult places a high value on the goodwill and the approval of friends, neighbours, family and colleagues at work. We fear ridicule, but we fear being shut out from the companionship of others even more. The most progressive and innovating adults are those who have confidence in their own judgment and who have less need for the approval of others.

Adults resent being pushed around and told what to do. We all want to be respected, intelligent, responsible human beings. We can accept help and advice only when doing so does not challenge our self-respect or our integrity as a person.

Be careful, too, not to violate the status and self-respect of your students, their satisfaction in their work or their social environment. Never embarrass a senior staff member in front of juniors, or vice versa.

Teach Just a Little

When you are trying to bring about some change, don't be in a hurry. Take time to listen before you start to introduce your new ideas. It is better to teach just a little and teach it well rather than to pour words over people ineffectively.

Arouse Interest Before You Start

We learn more easily when we are interested in the subject. Confidence and knowledge make us more receptive to learning. You will often find that a new skill will be picked up rapidly by persons who can already see when and where they will find a use for it.

Use Your Imagination

Don't take traditional methods for granted. Experiment with different training ways. Use your imagination—it's a powerful training tool.

Make Learning More Effective

Anyone who wishes to learn can be helped to improve the effectiveness of their learning.

- Work hard at maintaining attention and interest.

- Promote the recall of previously learned material.

- Break down large concepts into small learning units.

- Give continuous progress reports and encouragement.

- Allow sufficient practice time for becoming familiar with recently acquired skills and knowledge.

- Keep all your teaching material up to date and relevant.

Coping with Impatience

Learning new skills takes time. In many cases, constant practice over a long period may be required (learning how to be a good public speaker or a writer is likely to take years of practice). However, many students become frustrated when results do not come quickly.

Often the tutor has been to blame for setting unrealistic goals. To set an objective such as 'to teach management skills' and then to expect to produce a whole set of managers by bringing people together for one brief residential course would be ludicrous.

Signposts and Mileage Checks

A good way to start a training course is to discuss objectives—what both tutor and students are hoping to gain. This will help to establish realistic goals.

A good training course can be compared to a car journey. There should be a prearranged destination, adequate signposting, and regular map and mileage checks to make sure where you are and whether you're on the right road. Unfortunately, many tutors become overcommitted or do not have sufficient support services available. They need to be able to arrange adequate maintenance checks and repairs and for a sufficient fuel supply to keep the vehicle moving at a safe speed, allowing the passengers time to enjoy the scenery on the way.

As the training proceeds, you should be making regular evaluations and progress reports.

A 'course evaluation' at the very end of the course is of little use to the students. Regular checks should be made throughout. They provide a gauge as to the relevance and the effectiveness of the techniques that are being used—and a chance to change the course content, if necessary.

Nothing will sustain the adult in learning more than the feeling of 'getting somewhere'. Nothing is more frustrating than the absence of feedback or any indication of progress. Evaluations are important. A sense of achievement is one of our most satisfying experiences—especially achievement in learning.

After it's all over

People often have difficulty in readjusting to their jobs after a period of refresher study. This is caused by the difficulty of relating what they have learnt with what they are required to do. They may also have to contend with resentment from their colleagues who were not given the chance to attend the course.

Often, the adult learner who has been to such a course has been stimulated into trying to bring about changes too rapidly. This causes resentment, so that the new methods are resisted. This is very common when someone has been fired with enthusiasm after a period of study overseas.

A discussion on such problems at the conclusion of a training period can be well worthwhile.

"Ancora imparo" (Still I am learning). Michelangelo's favourite maxim.

2 SO YOU WANT TO BE A SUCCESSFUL TRAINER

After you have read this chapter you should be able to:

Formulate plans to be a more successful trainer

List the order of importance of various aids in learning

Question, plan, involve

- Why were you the successful applicant for your job?

- What does your boss expect of you?

- Read your job description. What is needed to satisfy its requirements?

- What are the standards for judging your performance?

- What are your strengths? Do you make the most of them?

Have regular discussions with key senior staff—they have the authority to make use of what you are teaching.

Look for the successes and failures of previous training sessions—find out the reasons for some of them.

Be ready to discuss people's problems as they see them. This is most important.

Concentrate on high-return areas—establish your credibility by selecting training projects that you know will be successful.

Follow up early successes to ensure they are fully exploited.

Your continuing success will depend on your being able to help management to reach their objectives—it is therefore essential for you to know at all times what those objectives are.

You must have direct communication with top management at all times.

Establish a regular feedback from all training activities. Evaluate regularly— never wait until the end of an exercise or course.

Be flexible and learn to profit from helpful criticism.

At the end of every training course assess what you have achieved. It is often hard to get honest 'face to face' comments. Ask participants to complete a reaction evaluation form (see fig. 11, p 34) or carry out a postal evaluation after they return home.

Helpful Hints

- Every person in every group is unique, with a different background and learning needs.

- Every training programme needs to be planned and developed to suit the varied needs of the group members.

- Assess the general standard of learning and knowledge so that you can begin at an appropriate level.

- Start with a topic that is familiar to the group, but add something new to stimulate curiosity and to arouse awareness of previously unrecognised needs.

- Move forward one step at a time.

- Adjust the size and difficulty of each step to the learners' ability.

- Be prepared to adjust each step, not only to the group as a whole but to any individual in the group—determine their readiness to learn, their familiarity with what has to be learned, and their speed of learning.

- Build each step on the preceding step—relate later learning experiences to earlier ones.

- Make sure you provide opportunities for all members to practise their newly acquired skills.

- Relate everything to a 'real-life' situation to show its meaning and application, and the variety of situations in which it can be used.

- Paint a clear picture of any changes you are attempting to make—explain the reasons for change.

- Be flexible in all your methods—if you really 'have your finger on the pulse' of the group, you should be able to feel when it is ready for a new learning experience.

- Try to put yourself in the other person's shoes and to imagine how you would feel, react, and behave if you were the person being trained.

- Try always to be tolerant and understanding.

- Encouragement and praise are among the cheapest and best of all training tools—they are also among the least used.

- Every course must have its clear objectives and expectations—the terms must have the same meaning for everyone.

- Remember that meanings are in people's minds—not in the words themselves.

- Keep your students hard at work for limited periods only—never for indefinite, unspecified stretches. Allow enough time for creative thinking, to produce worthwhile ideas.

- Remember that lengthy periods of physical inactivity in the confines of a room do not usually encourage creative thinking. Set deadlines and try to keep to them.

- Imagination can play an important role in learning. ('Suppose you had just been made Prime Minister, what would you do . . .?'')

- Try to make every member feel 'involved'—to feel they can share experiences freely, without fear of 'losing face'.

- Exercises should be seen to be worthwhile and relevant—preferably ending with useful, practicable recommendations.

- Develop a working climate which encourages constructive self-criticism. ('How can I do better next time?')

- Regular evaluations will help to build great empathy among the course members and will allow for any changes in direction that may become necessary.

- Involve everyone in experience-sharing, but make sure comments are concise so that everybody has a chance to participate.

- What the listeners think the speaker said is more important than what the speaker thinks he said.

- Don't forget that the traditional lecture is probably the most ineffective way of all to teach.

- Real experiences are the most effective.

- Words are the least effective teaching aid.

THE VALUE OF VARIOUS AIDS TO LEARNING

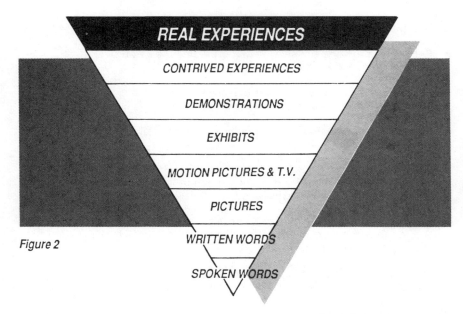

Figure 2

"Hearing is with the ears, but listening is with the mind."

3 PLANNING TRAINING

After you have read this chapter you should be able to:

Analyse your trainees and their jobs
Identify their training needs
Write clear training objectives
Decide on content of the course
Select the best training ways for your course
Prepare a worksheet and lesson plan
Evaluate your training

There are three stages to successful training:

A. Detailed planning
B. Adequate preparation
C. Lively presentation

Figure 3 outlines a training plan with the elements of the training process arranged in a logical sequence. If you work through these systematically, your training should be more effective. Remember that the more costly the training, the greater the effort you should put into the analysis and planning.

Any training plan should start with a good briefing from the initiator of the plan. Initiators are usually administrators or managers who set the goals to be achieved. They must be kept informed throughout the training because they are responsible for approving the training budget.

The first tasks are to analyse the job requirements, carry out a trainee analysis and decide on their training needs. You are then able to determine the training objectives. See Figure 4.

Training Process

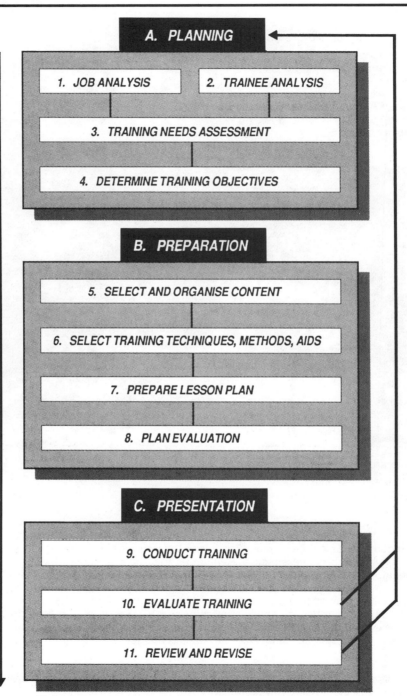

A. PLANNING

1. JOB ANALYSIS   2. TRAINEE ANALYSIS

3. TRAINING NEEDS ASSESSMENT

4. DETERMINE TRAINING OBJECTIVES

B. PREPARATION

5. SELECT AND ORGANISE CONTENT

6. SELECT TRAINING TECHNIQUES, METHODS, AIDS

7. PREPARE LESSON PLAN

8. PLAN EVALUATION

C. PRESENTATION

9. CONDUCT TRAINING

10. EVALUATE TRAINING

11. REVIEW AND REVISE

Figure 3

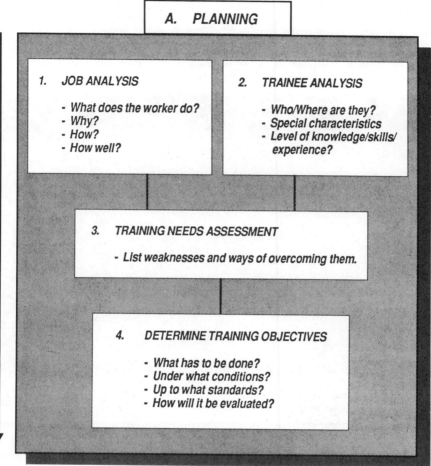

A.   PLANNING

1.   JOB ANALYSIS

- **What does the worker do?**
- **Why?**
- **How?**
- **How well?**

2.   TRAINEE ANALYSIS

- **Who/Where are they?**
- **Special characteristics**
- **Level of knowledge/skills/ experience?**

3.   TRAINING NEEDS ASSESSMENT

- **List weaknesses and ways of overcoming them.**

4.   DETERMINE TRAINING OBJECTIVES

- **What has to be done?**
- **Under what conditions?**
- **Up to what standards?**
- **How will it be evaluated?**

Figure 4

1 Job Analysis

To carry out a job analysis start by looking at the job description. Use it as a guide only and don't take it for granted that everything in the job description is being done.

List all tasks required for the job.

Tasks should be expressed in terms of what people do, **not** what gets done or accomplished.

Complete a worksheet for job analysis for each task. See Figure 5. Start by listing tasks in the WHAT column; then complete the other columns. The HOW WELL column is the most difficult but try to set standards.

A completed job analysis has many uses besides the planning of training. It can be used as the basis for writing a manual, for counselling staff or for reorganising supervisory or work relationships.

WORKSHEET FOR JOB ANALYSIS (Separate sheet for each task)			
What has to be done (Action verb + object)	Why To produce or achieve what?	How	How Well What is a good job?
To.....	In order to	With whom?	Quantity
		Where?	Outputs required?
(See list of behavioural objective verbs, fig. 8, page 27)		Process or Procedure	What results are needed?
		Using what tools/ equipment and facilities?	Quality What standards are required?

Figure 5

2 Trainee Analysis

Characteristics of trainees that may influence your training

1. **Physical characteristics**
   Age and sex of trainees, size of group, location of training

2. **Educational characteristics**
   Language, vocabulary, knowledge, skills, learning style trainees are familiar with, etc.

3. **Psychological characteristics**
   Prejudices, attitudes, beliefs, values, interests, motivation, norms, etc.

4. **Socio-economic characteristics**
   Status, occupation, authority

5. **Working experiences**
   On-the-job training, etc.

How can you collect this information?

— Interviews, questionnaires, group meetings, conversations, letters from trainees, interviews with colleagues, supervisors, etc.

— Observation of trainees at work, tests, case studies, role playing, reports, records of work, etc.

Usually a mixture of methods is best. Be tactful and gather only the information you need. Don't be too inquisitive. Figure 6 is a suggested guide for gathering data for a trainee analysis.

Categories	Detailed Information		
	Essential	Useful	Not Necessary
Education/training/experience			
Sex			
Age			
Occupation			
Affiliations/special interests/aptitudes			
Knowledge of subject			
Language			
Attitudes, beliefs			
Authority			

DATA FOR TRAINEE ANALYSIS

Figure 6

Possible Headings for a Trainee Analysis Form

1. **Size** of group
2. **Sex** ratio
3. **Age** groups
   a. 15–25
   b. 26–35
   c. 36–45
   d. 46–
4. **Location** — urban/rural (percentages)
5. **Education** — university, secondary, primary (percentages)
6. **Positions** — occupations
7. **Years of experience** in present position

8. Most **important tasks** trainees perform

    1. _____
    2. _____
    3. _____
    4. _____

9. **Knowledge of trainees** about their work — good, fair, poor
10. Trainees' feelings and beliefs about their job

3 Training Needs Assessment

When you have completed the job analysis and the trainee analysis, you should be able to assess their current knowledge and skills and so decide on their training needs. Figure 7 shows a suggested form to record these findings.

TRAINEE'S PRESENT KNOWLEDGE AND NEEDS					
Job requirement	Trainee's current knowledge and skills				
	Excellent	Good	Fair	Poor	Nil
1.					
2.					
3.					
4.					
etc.					
Training needs (evident from the above information)					
1.					
2.					
3.					
4.					
5.					
etc.					

Figure 7

4 Training Objectives

A training objective for a particular group is a target or an achievement. It should specify the type of change that is expected, when it will occur, and finally, how it will be measured to determine its level of success.

In other words, it describes what trainees should be able to do at the end of their training that they could not do previously. Therefore trainee analysis and training needs assessment should be carried out well before training objectives are written.

An objective must

— describe the final results
— be specific and precise
— describe a change that is measurable or observed
— list criteria against which success can be measured or judged
— mention all the essential conditions under which the results can be achieved
— specify an end point

Some Commonly Used Behavioural Objective Words			
classify	differentiate	Identify	prepare
construct	discuss	indicate	specify
define	distinguish	integrate	state
describe	establish	list	trace
designate	evaluate	name	
determine	explain	practise	

Figure 8

ABCD on Writing Training Objectives

Before you start writing objectives, consider the following:

A. **Audience** — Who are you going to train?
   You should know the participants' or trainees' background.

B. **Behaviour** — What type of change do you expect?
   You should be able to describe the desired change and explain its advantages.

C. **Condition** — When and under what conditions do you expect this change to occur? e.g. "Improved performance should be evident after eight hours of demonstration and practice and a 40 min. lecture."

D. **Degree** — How much change do you expect and how will you find out? See p. 33.

Example:
Agricultural instructors, after one week's training, will be able to:
— Identify brown plant hoppers (Nilaparvata lugens).
— Explain the life cycle to farmers and time of treatment for prevention and control.
— Identify "hopper burn" in rice crops.
— Demonstrate safety measures when mixing and spraying insecticides.
— Mix the correct amount of insecticide for control of brown plant hoppers.
— Demonstrate to farmers how to spray a crop for prevention and control of brown plant hoppers.

B.   PREPARATION

5.   SELECT AND ORGANISE CONTENT

- Study sources of information.
- Decide on content.
- Organise content in logical sequence.

6.   SELECT TRAINING TECHNIQUES, METHODS, AIDS

- Decide on appropriate techniques.
- Select suitable methods.
- Decide on training aids required.

7.   PREPARE LESSON PLANS

- Decide how each lesson is to be presented.
- Set out each lesson step by step.
- Allocate times for each activity.

8.   PLAN EVALUATION

- Decide on information required.
- Decide when this should be collected.
- Study methods of gathering information.
- Select method to be used.
- Prepare questions which have to be answered.

Figure 9

5 Select and Organise Content of Course

After analysing the training objectives decide on the content of the course. This should cover the detailed knowledge, skills and attitudes required on topics that support the objectives.

When selecting content:

— remember the purpose of the training
— prepare an outline of the content
— classify content into

(a) **what must be known** (skills and knowledge that are essential to do the basic tasks.)
(b) **what should be known** (skills and knowledge needed in order to perform additional or related tasks.)
(c) **what could be known** (skills and knowledge that relate to the job, but are not essential.)

— build up a content selection worksheet. Figure 10 shows some suggested headings for this worksheet.

CONTENT SELECTION WORKSHEET OBJECTIVES - (Write training objective here)									
What needs to be known					What needs to be performed				
Topic	Details	Must	Should	Could	Topic	Details	Must	Should	Could

Figure 10

Organising Content

The content should be put in logical order, or sequence. Certain parts of the content will have to be understood before other subjects can be introduced. Logical order will produce faster learning.

Contents can be organised in different ways:
1. **Job performance order**. Training is given in the order in which tasks are performed.
2. **Problem order**. Training is given in the order you would use to solve a problem.
3. **Simple to complex**. Training is given according to what the trainee needs to know before more complex ideas are introduced.

When the contents of the training course have been selected, classified and arranged in suitable order, you can then decide on the training methods to use to make your training enjoyable and effective.

6 Which Training Ways Should You Use?

To transfer knowledge, use:

Group discussions (questions and answers)
Group or individual exercises
Lectures (with handouts)
Forums
Panel discussions
Films, videos, etc.

To practise problem solving, use:

Case studies
Brain-storming
Discussion groups
Exercises etc.

To develop skills, use:

Demonstrations for manual skills
Role playing for interpersonal skills
Peer teaching
Programmed instructions etc.

To change attitudes, use:

Debates
Displays
Role playing (for clarifying how others feel)
Group discussion (for group attitudes)
Individual exercises
Demonstrations
Campaigns etc.

7 Worksheet and Lesson Plan

Lesson plans and worksheets should list the steps and activities and equipment needed in training sessions. Before a lesson plan is written, the following questions should be answered:

What training methods will be most suitable?
What style of presentation is best?
How will new information be introduced?
What audio-visual aids will be needed?

A lesson should be planned by writing an outline of what is to be taught and the methods to be used. Times should be allocated for the various activities. The places where training is to take place and all equipment needed should be checked also. Time should be allowed for summarising the main points at the end of a lesson and also for distributing any necessary handouts.

Throughout all training, time should be allowed for monitoring progress and understanding by discussions, reviews, group exercises and short tests/examinations.

Suggested headings for lesson preparation

Title
Content
Training ways
Desired result from participants (knowledge, skill, attitudes)
Location, seating, etc.
Equipment and materials required (teaching aids)
Time in training room
Time on outside activities

Suggested Lesson Plan

1. Review previous lessons.
2. Introduce the subject. Tell class the content of the lesson and desired results.
3. Lead in from previous training.
4. Obtain student involvement. Let them share their experiences.
5. Lecture with demonstrations, films, models, etc.
6. Student activity — visits, practicals, role playing, debating.
7. Discussion or reports — arising from activities.
8. Summarise main points.
9. Outline next lesson plan.

8 Plan Evaluation

Why evaluate?

The questions most often asked about any training programme are:
  (a) How effective is it?
  (b) Is it worth the money?
  (c) How can the training be improved?

Evaluation of the training course can help provide answers to these questions.

What is evaluation?

In simple terms, evaluation can be defined as:
"A means of identifying the strengths and weaknesses of a particular activity or programme with the aim of making a decision about it."

The decision may be to improve, expand, modify or cancel it — or even to leave the programme unchanged if it is thought to be effective as it stands.

What are the main types of evaluation?

There are four main types of evaluation:

1. Reaction evaluation
This measures the reaction of the trainees themselves to the training programme or any of its components.

2. Learning evaluation
This measures change in the trainee's knowledge, attitudes and practices. A pre-training test (pretest) is compared with post-training test (post-test) results.

3. Performance evaluation
This measures how the trainee's job performance has altered after a period of time as a result of training. Performance before training is compared with that after training.

4. Impact evaluation
This measures the effectiveness of the training by assessing the type and degree of change which the trainees have had on the organisation or target group with which they work.

If all these four types of evaluation are carried out effectively they will show whether or not the training programme is effective or if the money has been well spent. They will also provide information on which areas of the training programme should be improved.

In reality however, it is rarely possible to use all four types of evaluation due to limited resources.

The trainer is responsible for deciding which type of evaluation, if any, will be conducted. The following five examples are given as guidelines for various situations.

Situation 1

If you want **quantitative data** such as the number of courses offered, number of trainees being trained, the duration of training, the training budget, etc. no formal evaluation needs to be conducted. A **report** with statistics about the training programme should be sufficient. It should include:

1. Title and topic of the course
2. Duration and dates
3. Number of trainees attending
4. Total budget used for training

(A training report should also include information on objectives of the programme, activities undertaken, outputs and evaluation results.)

Situation 2

If you want to find out whether or not the trainees are **satisfied with the course** and why, or if the training programme needs to be improved and how this could be done, a **reaction evaluation** should be carried out.

To obtain the trainee's reaction to the course, ask general questions such as:

1. What did you like most about the course?
2. What did you dislike most about the course?
3. Did the course achieve its objectives?
4. How could it be improved?

These questions can be asked informally or set out as formal questionnaires for each trainee to complete. The latter is often preferable because the personal reactions of all trainees can be obtained with the minimum influence from their peers. On the other hand, daily informal discussions are very useful because you get immediate feedback.

This information can also be obtained by asking trainees to complete a form such as the one shown in Figure 11. Various aspects of the course are rated on a given scale.

REACTION EVALUATION FORM

Title and Topic of Course_____ Date_____

To help the organisers of the training programme improve their course, please rate the training on a scale by drawing a circle around the appropriate number.

	Good	Fair	Poor
	3	2	1
1. Value of this training in relation to my job	3	2	1
2. Presentation method used	3	2	1
3. Training facilities	3	2	1
4. Opportunity for participation	3	2	1
5. Value of handouts	3	2	1
6. Duration of training	3	2	1

Figure 11

If you want to find out whether or not the trainees were able to achieve the **training objectives**, or whether there is any change in their knowledge, attitude and practices as a result of the training, a **learning evaluation** should be conducted. This should include pre- and post- training tests.

To test how much the trainees have learned during the course, various tests can be used e.g.

3.1 Essay
e.g. Describe the advantages and limitations of teaching by the lecture method.

3.2 Short answer questions
e.g. Answer the following questions:
What is learning evaluation?
When should it be used?
How can it be conducted?

3.3 Completion of sentences
e.g. Complete the following:
(. . . . . .) evaluation is used to determine the ultimate success of the training by ascertaining whether or not the problem has been solved and if so, if it was due to the training.

3.4 True or false questions
e.g. Performance evaluation is used to determine whether the training objectives have been achieved. True/False (Yes/No answers are also a quick way of finding how much trainees have learned.)

3.5 Multiple choice questions
e.g. If you want to teach someone a skill, it is best to:
(a) Show a film of someone doing the job.
(b) Give a lecture on how to do it.
(c) Demonstrate on a model.
(d) Make the trainee do the job with someone supervising each step.

Please write the correct answer (a,b,c or d).

The above are examples of some common forms of tests for knowledge. For attitudes and skills, sample tests are as follows:

Test for attitude
Please circle the abbreviation that best fits your opinion.

Meaning of abbreviations SA = Strongly agree, A = Agree, D = Disagree, SD = Strongly disagree

1. Smoking in public buses is reasonable behaviour SA   A   D   SD

2. Democracy is the best form of government SA   A   D   SD

Test for skill

The trainer or an observer fills in a check list as the trainee performs the required skill. For example: **To test if the trainee can set up an overhead projector.**

Place a tick (✓) according to what the trainee does.

		Correct	Wrong
1.	Make sure there are no distracting light sources.	( )	( )
2.	Find the nearest power source and test to see that it works.	( )	( )
3.	Get a suitable table (height and rigidity are important) and place it in position.	( )	( )
4.	Place overhead projector on table.	( )	( )
5.	Plug in projector making sure the cord is safely out of the way of the audience. (It is a good idea to first wrap the projector cord around the leg of the table. This prevents the projector crashing to the floor if someone trips on the cord.)	( )	( )
6.	Turn on electric power.	( )	( )
7.	Check that the bulb is working.	( )	( )
8.	Set up the screen, adjusting it to get a 45 degree angle to the projector light beam.	( )	( )
9.	Place a transparency on projector, and focus.	( )	( )
10.	Adjust table so that the picture fills up the screen.	( )	( )
11.	Move around the room and sit down in various positions to check that the screen can be seen clearly from all parts of the room.	( )	( )

To measure change in a trainee's skill, a test should be given just before the training programme and another just after it is completed.

Situation 4

If you want to study the **job performance** of the trainees after their return to work, carry out a **performance evaluation**. Again, this should include pretests and post-tests of the trainees' performance.

To evaluate the performance of trainees after their return to work, use:
   (a) Observation forms
   (b) Questionnaires
   (c) Details of work output

Example
"After completion of training, the trainee is expected to be able to type in English at a speed of at least 30 words per minute without errors." An observation form to evaluate this performance could be set out as follows:

Name of typist _____

Date _____

1. Typing a given text in English.   No. of mistakes _____
2. Time spent in typing   _____ min._____ secs.
3. Speed of typing   _____ words/min.
4. Evaluation   _____
5. Remarks (and possible recommendations) _____

Another way to assess the typist's performance would be to check the quality of randomly selected work. A speed test should be carried out prior to training as it is only **change** in performance that can be attributed to the training.

Performance evaluation should be given after definite periods of time — say two weeks, three months and six months after training.

Situation 5

If you want to find whether the **problems** in an organisation or community have been solved when the trainees return to work and whether this is due to the training, carry out an **impact evaluation**. This should include pre- and post- assessment of conditions and indicators.

Baseline data should be collected before training starts. Evaluation to determine the impact of training should normally be carried out within the year following training.

This is the most difficult and expensive type of evaluation to carry out. Therefore it needs to be planned carefully and a budget allocated before the training starts.

Example

Population education programme
Bandumi village had a problem of high population growth. One of the older villagers had considerable influence in the village and had expressed concern over the problem. It was proposed that she should receive training in population concepts and family planning. Before this was done, the following data was collected (the baseline indicators).

   (a) Total population of the community
   (b) Total number of births per year
   (c) Total number of deaths per year
   (d) Number of people leaving the community
   (e) Number of people entering the community

This information allowed calculation of the growth rate of the community before training was carried out i.e. $(b-c) + (e-d)/a$.

One year after training, the same type of data could be collected again. If there is a decline in the population growth rate, it may be the result of the work of the community leader who has taught family planning methods. It may, however, be nothing to do with the training and could be the result of:

(1) Outward migration of people from the village
(2) A sudden increase in the availability of contraceptives
(3) Other factors

All possible factors should be considered before it can be concluded that the change is the result of training the community leader.

The above situations involve only one type of evaluation (situation 2, 3, 4 and 5) or no formal evaluation (situation 1, which is covered by a report). However, in most cases, decisions are rarely as simple or clear-cut as these and it may be necessary to conduct more than one type of evaluation.

```
┌─────────────────────────────────┐
│  C.   PRESENTATION              │
└─────────────────────────────────┘

   9.   CONDUCT TRAINING

        - Keep to your lesson plans.
        - Use a variety of methods.
        - Encourage participation.
        - Use demonstrations, models, visual aids.


   10.  EVALUATE TRAINING

        - Conduct planned evaluation.
        - Summarise results.
        - Write evaluation report.


   11.  REVIEW AND REVISE

        - Summarise training.
        - Review in the light of evaluations.
        - Discuss with other trainers involved.
        - Revise to improve relevance.
```

Figure 12

9 Conduct Training

To be a good trainer you require experience and skill. Experience comes with practice, and skill with evaluations. Here are some helpful hints:

1. Get to know your students — their needs, their ambitions, their humour.

2. The discipline of going back to basics is a valuable learning experience.

3. Little of what we passively listen to is remembered. People learn best by doing things. The more participation you have in your training the better it will be.

4. The more variety you can get into your training the more interesting it will be.

39

5. A good basis for training is "tell — show — ask — discuss — do — review".

6. A good demonstration will save you a lot of talking.

7. Allow plenty of time for trainees to practise new skills.

8. Objective evaluations are important and must be taken notice of. The trainer must be ready to change the content of his course and his training methods—he must be flexible in his attitudes.

9. Use imagination when designing a programme.

10. Make your training lively — make it interesting and make it fun.

10 Evaluate Training

The four main types of evaluation i.e.
    (a) Reaction evaluation
    (b) Learning evaluation
    (c) Performance evaluation
    (d) Impact evaluation

are discussed in Section 8 of this chapter at the planning stage. (See p. 33)

Each should have been considered for evaluation of the effectiveness of the training and the most appropriate type(s) planned and prepared before training began.

When the evaluation is completed, results should be reported for further discussion and action. The most important action to take after a training evaluation is to decide whether to cancel, improve or modify future training programmes.

11 Review and Revise

Training should be dynamic. Each group is different so make your training flexible and relevant to your participants' needs.

Constantly review, revise and experiment with your training methods — it's the only way to keep your training fresh, vibrant and interesting.

"The battle cry for this decade will be performance, productivity and accountability."

4 MANAGING TRAINING

After you have read this chapter you should be able to:

Prepare your own training check lists

Organise residential courses

Just as the crew of an aircraft has a detailed checklist of instruments to check before take-off so should trainers before starting training.

A new trainer should prepare his or her own list, then add to or amend it after each course. This makes planning future sessions easier and builds confidence that courses will be a success.

This subject is divided into five suggested checklists.
1. **Before** planning a training course
2. **Planning** the training
3. **Preparation** for course
4. **Residential course**
5. **Evaluation**

Finally, there is a summary table of the main issues to be considered in training activities.

1. Before Planning a Training Course

— How does training fit into national and departmental goals?
— Why is training needed?
— Who is going to pay?

— Who has the authority to approve expenditure, travel, participants' absence from work?
— What is the training policy?
— Who is to be trained?
— How many people are to be trained?
— What are their backgrounds? Do they have a job description containing title, function, objectives, acceptable standards of performance and responsibilities?
— What are their needs? Do you need to carry out a job analysis?
— What do they need to be taught?
— What resources have you?
— How much time is available?
— How are trainees to be selected?

2. Planning the Training

A. Objectives
— Decide on training objectives and write them down.
— Be specific and precise.
— Describe the desired result.
— Describe a change you can measure or observe.
— What criteria can you use to judge success?
— List conditions where results can be achieved.
— How will you know when you have achieved your objectives?
— What new tasks will the trainees be able to do?

B. Methods
— Where are you going to carry out training?
— What sort of training are you going to carry out — job related training, training to overcome a problem or teaching new techniques or new skills?
— What topics are to be covered?
  Both top management and participants should be involved in deciding on the course content and both should be consulted during the course.
— How are you going to teach topics?
  Aim to get as much participation as possible.
— Design course and break it up into learning experiences.

3. Preparation For Course

— Decide on the training methods you will use.
— Select instructors, contact them to see if they are available and brief them on what is required.
— What training aids are needed? Check the rooms to see if electricity is available, if you can darken the room for films, etc. Check on availability of training aids such as blackboards, paper pads, overhead projectors, film projectors, white boards, etc.
— Are the rooms suitable for training?
— Are they quiet?

— Can the trainer be heard easily in all parts of the room?
— Is lighting adequate?
— Can rooms be adequately ventilated and air-conditioned or heated if necessary?
— What seating arrangement is to be used — circular, U-shaped or square?
— Do you need tables for writing?
— Recheck that all necessary equipment will be available when required and in good working order.
— Prepare lesson plans but be flexible, allowing time for extra discussions or more practical work.
— Prepare handouts.
— Are you going to print proceedings of the course? If so, contact reporters, typist, editors, printers, etc.

4. Residential Course

— Prepare a budget.
— Book accommodation for participants and any visiting instructors.
— Make travel arrangements.
— Organise meals, tea and coffee breaks.
— Prepare information for support staff, instructors, management and servicing people such as caterers, cooks, audio visual technicians, librarians, caretakers and drivers. All necessary instructions and details of number of trainees, times of arrival, etc. should be given in writing.
— Prepare printed information for trainees. This should include:

> — A message welcoming course members.
> — Outline of objectives (what is expected from trainees).
> — Detailed timetable. Make sure you allow adequate time for participants to get from place to place.
> — Statement on costs, also information on any sponsorships or subsidies that might be available.
> — List of course members and where they come from.
> — Map of campus layout showing meeting rooms, office, sleeping accommodation, toilet facilities, bus stops, shops, etc.
> — Note of any relevant training area regulations.
> — Advice on possible health problems. Where to go, whom to see, likely costs and payment procedures.
> — Names and whereabouts of persons who are available when help is needed.
> — Note on room-cleaning arrangements, laundry facilities (where and when available) and bed-linen changes.
> — Library hours and rules.
> — Note on recreation facilities — types and times available, rules, and any charges to be paid.
> — Advice on locking rooms and putting valuables into safe keeping.
> — Location of nearest shopping facilities. (Availability of writing materials, toilet gear, stamps, "snacks", etc.)
> — Correct postal address for trainees. Where to collect and post mail, local postal charges.
> — Mealtimes, times for morning and afternoon teas.
> — Person to contact for any special diet requirements.

— Public transport services — where to get buses/trains, their
frequency and cost.
— Location of various churches, temples or mosques, approximate
distances from training centre and times of prayers and services.
— Nearest banking facilities.
— Name and location of person with overall responsibility for
organising and administering course. Times when he/she is
available.
— Advice on how return-travel arrangements are to be confirmed.
— Trainees will also appreciate tourist-type publicity brochures and a
map of local area.

5. Evaluation

How will you know if training has been successful?
        — How effective has it been?
        — Was it worth the money expended?
        — How could a similar course be improved?

How will you evaluate? How often?
Which of the following four methods will you use?

        1. Reaction evaluation
        2. Learning evaluation
        3. Performance evaluation
        4. Impact evaluation. See Chapter 3 for examples.

TRAINING CHECK LIST			
	Specific answers required, persons to be contacted, etc.	Date to be completed	Done ✓
1. Who approves training? manages training?			
2. Who are the trainees? trainers? support staff			
3. Why is there a need for training? What is the training policy?			
4. How much money is available? What is the length of the course?			
5. What are the course objectives? What subjects are to be taught? What jobs are to be done? Who will do them?			

	Specific answers required, persons to be contacted, etc.	Date to be completed	Done ✓
6. When should planning be done? When should preparation be done? When is the presentation? When will the evaluation be done?			
7. Where will the training be carried out? Which rooms? laboratory? workshop? fields? others?			
8. Who will do what? when? where? why? how?			
9. What materials are needed? List equipment, supplies, audiovisuals, handouts, etc.			
10. Have all trainees been given clear written instructions about the course?			
11. Have you double-checked arrangements for accommodation? catering? travel?			
12. Have you evaluated the course?			
13. Have you written a report and completed the budget?			
14. Have you written to thank instructors, hostel managers, etc.?			

Figure 13

5 PARTICIPATIVE TRAINING

Participative training is a "learning through sharing and doing" activity. It is often called "discovery", "experiential" or "action" learning.

Participants are involved in activities designed to share experiences and discover new information. It can be used with groups of varying sizes.

Basically it is discovering one's needs and sharing knowledge about satisfying them, while developing interpersonal skills.

Participative training can be a very effective training method because we are more likely to remember a solution we have worked out for ourselves than one thought out for us. Also we are more likely to act on decisions we have made for ourselves.

Some Examples of Participative Training
- Discussion groups
- Competitive groups
- Role playing groups
- Simulation exercises
- Workshops
- Seminars
- Forums

— Tutorials
— Contests
— Quizzes
— Debates

Environment

— Arrange the room for interaction.
— Round tables take the emphasis off the trainer and help promote participation.
— Tables set up to form a square, or chairs set in a circle, establish equality between participants and trainer and help promote group discussion.
— U shapes, too, promote interaction, but establish the trainer as authority.

Getting Started

— **Allow time for getting acquainted**. This helps build a climate of trust and makes it easier for participants to relax and respond.
— **Start off by dividing the group into pairs**.
— Select a "comfortable" topic, preferably non-controversial e.g. "What interests have you outside your work?" Get the pairs to discuss the topic and then ask individuals to report on what they learned about their partners.

Chaining is a good warm-up technique. In chaining, the trainer aims to get a series of responses, each of which leads to the next. Here a controversial subject is best e.g. "Agricultural extension services have failed the farmer" or "Trade is more important than aid."

Get each person to stand and speak for one minute. When the time is up, the next person must continue in logical sequence — preferably not repeating previous arguments.

Triads
When the group is familiar with pairing exercises, form groups of three. The groups should be asked to discuss questions that everyone can answer e.g. "What is the biggest problem you have in your job?" Appoint the person in the middle to act as chairperson and later to report findings to the full meeting.

Allow thinking time
When stating a problem or asking a question, ask participants to jot down a few notes before they work in groups.

Dividing into working groups

1. The traditional way
After counting the number of participants, decide on the number of groups and the size of each group. For example, if there are 21 participants and you want three groups, you can count off groups of seven or number them off, "One, two, three. One, two, three, etc. All the "Ones" here, the "Twos" there and the "Threes" in this corner." Then send groups off to elect their own leaders.

2. The democratic way

Hand out a sheet of paper. Ask participants to write down the name of one person they would like as a leader. Collect them and count to see who are the most popular choices. The winners of the ballot come forward and draw lots to see who selects first. (Break off 3 match sticks at different lengths and let each leader have a draw. The person with the longest has first choice, and so on.)

They take turns at selecting participants for their group.

Write the names in each group on a blackboard or use an overhead projector so all can see.

3. The autocratic way

Prior to the activity, the trainer selects the participants to make up balanced groups. Lists are printed and handed out.

Guidelines

After the groups have been established, set up training guidelines. Make the rules as democratic as possible. For example:

- There will be no rank in the training room — all are equal.
- Say what you honestly think.
- Only one person to speak at a time.
- Make a special effort to listen carefully to all discussions.
- Be brief with your comments.
- Anything said in groups is confidential. Only group conclusions will be reported to the whole meeting.
- Be punctual and try to attend every session.

Use of Participative Methods

- To identify, explore, and seek solutions to problems.
- To develop plans for action.
- Where necessary, to change attitudes through an amicable examination of the evidence.
- To develop leadership skills.
- As a supplementary technique in many types of training.

Advantages

- Groups pool experiences, abilities, and knowledge to reach recognised goals.
- Allows every member to participate fully.
- Can establish a democratic consensus.
- Can stimulate a desire to learn and to share.
- Often one individual's enthusiasm can stimulate the whole group.

Limitations

- Can be time consuming, particularly if persons with strong convictions or widely different backgrounds are involved.
- Preliminary exercises are needed before serious group activity is possible.

Requirements

- A skilled chairperson (or leader) is needed to prevent the more dominant members from taking over the group.
- Participants should sit in a circle or rectangle, in an informal, relaxed atmosphere that is free from noise and other distractions.
- "Face-to-face" discussion is essential.
- Discussion is usually less restrained when a group is small. The effectiveness of group discussion may decline when there are more than seven people in a group or when there are more than 30 in the workshop. (A workshop of 28, for example, could be appropriately divided into four groups of seven and if these were balanced in terms of age, personality and experience, conditions would be ideal for training.)
- Each group should appoint a chairperson (or leader) and a reporter.

Preparation and Procedure

- Be sure your instructions to groups are clear, precise, and preferably, written (for easy reference). For example:

  "Topic . . . .
  It is now 2 p.m.
  You have 1 hour in which to

- appoint a reporter

- discuss the topic and bring down recommendations to solve the problems.

  It is suggested that you

- break the topic into workable "bites"

- arrange your recommendations in their order of priority

- appoint a spokesperson to report your findings to the full meeting

- arrange for your reporter to hand the tutor a copy of your findings.

  Report back at 3 p.m."

- Start off with exercises which are interesting, topical and appropriate for the group.

Hints

- Group co-operation should be stressed at an early stage. A good approach is to introduce a controversial topic for discussion but without any guidelines. Such a discussion inevitably grows heated — it is not always relevant; there is disagreement on procedures; personality clashes occur; and one or two people monopolise all the available time.

  Ask the group to discuss what happened without a chairperson and rules. Having experienced the difficulties of unguided discussion, most people will be interested in learning the mechanics of group interaction, and later discussions will be more productive.

  Observation Exercise. A helpful exercise is to split a large group into two working parties, one of which discusses a controversial topic while the other sits **silently** and observes. Brief the groups separately, keeping the briefing simple. For example, the observers could be told:

- "Each of you is to sit behind a member of the working group, but not close enough to cause distraction."

- "Draw a simple diagram to record the discussion pattern."

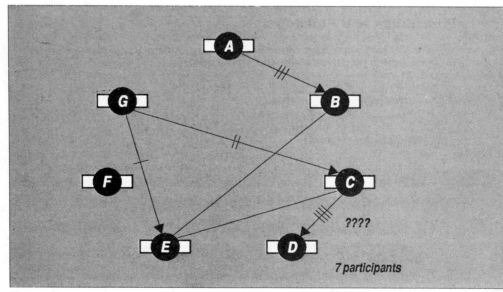

Figure 14

The lines in this example show that A spoke to B three times, C asked four questions of D, and so on. This provides a general picture of the group's most active members.

Encourage the observers to identify various types of behaviour. They should be able to identify which member

asks the most questions
provides the best information
acts as guide
talks about the group
seeks and encourages ideas
settles the arguments
is content just to follow
keeps the group happy
imposes his opinion on the rest
does not contribute at all

Ask for comments on any other interesting behaviour, e.g.
"Have you noticed any changes in the relationship between various members?"
"Has the group's attitude as a whole changed?"
"Has an obvious leader emerged?"
"Did any real plan evolve?"

The main points to observe here are the progress of the group as a whole and the interaction of its members.

At the end of the observation exercise, ask the groups to reverse their roles i.e. the observation group now becomes the discussion group.

Set the new discussion group a topic that is relevant to group discussion. For example: "What conclusions can be drawn about the effectiveness of group discussion?" or "How can the workings of a discussion group be improved?" or "What are the advantages and disadvantages of formality in groups?"

At the conclusion of this exercise, bring the groups together for a general discussion. Draw up some practical guidelines that can be applied to future sessions e.g.

■ One member should not be allowed to dominate

■ Any shy members must be encouraged

■ Private conversations hinder group discussion and should be discouraged.

Observations on Group Dynamics

■ The size of the group is important. Small groups encourage more active participation.

■ A group's effectiveness depends upon the personalities of its members.

- Its effectiveness also depends on the style of leadership.

- Social pressures in a group can be very strong and, if not closely watched, can hinder progress.

- Any adverse criticism must relate to an **idea** and not to its originator. (Personal criticism can lead to the "injured" member withdrawing from any further discussion.)

- A video replay can provide a useful analysis of group dynamics. When participants become accustomed to having a camera in the room, they will start to act naturally. Two "operators" will be needed — one as the cameraman and the other to maintain an accurate time sequence, so that any particular section can be found easily in a replay. The filming should concentrate on wide-angle shots of the whole group, but the occasional close-up will highlight a point and identify the "doodlers", the "chatterers", or the "dozers".

Participative training is a powerful training tool. It is learning through sharing and doing. But don't forget when you are talking you will not be learning.

"In teaching there should be no class distinctions". Confucius.

6 TRAINING WAYS

After you have read this chapter you should be able to:

Identify a wider range of training methods

Select more effective training ways for your courses and workshops

Establish a rapport with your trainees

Which Method?

There are many different ways to teach. Too many tutors have too few tools in their teaching kits.

A particular group was asked to list and then to classify all the teaching methods they could think of. Figure 15 shows the list they made. Do you agree with it and with their classifications? Can you think of any methods they have left out? Are any of them wrongly classified?

Variety is Important

Be sure your programme is flexible. Build "flexibility" into the training. Provide some uncertainty, some variety, some competition, and some entertainment. We learn best when we enjoy our learning and are spurred into competing. It has been said that "Variety is the spice of life" — the same is true for training.

TEACHING AIDS	
Active	*Inactive*
Spoken Seminar, group discussion, evaluating, question period, conversing, simulation exercise, interview	Lecture, visit, observation session, forum, telephone calls, song, role playing, conference, debating, panel discussions, radio programme, talk, questions, suggestion, slogans, poetry, demonstrations, coaching, home visiting, taped programmes, workshop, tutorials
Written Assignment, directed reading, survey, games, projects, crossword puzzles, 'filling-in' forms, problem solving	Letters, brochures, bulletins, manuals, circulars, leaflets, case studies, newsletters, reports, regulations, books, magazines, newspapers, 'filling-in' blanks
Visual Constructing visual aids, models, amassing a collection, actual object, display	Sighting real objects, slides, diagrams, cartoon, blackboard, graphs, chart, transparencies, overhead projectors, models, displays, photographs, poster, wall newspapers, maps, puppet show, exhibitions, trade fairs, field tours, drama, epidiascope, drawings, flannelgraph, display board, magnetic board, albums, histogram, samples, observations, advertisements, symbols, picture story
Audio-visual Video-tape recorders	Demonstration, tape-slide shows, filmstrips (with commentaries), display, films, cartoon, field day, 'tours', closed-circuit television

Figure 15

Mental Peaks

The good teacher exploits the naturally occurring concentration peaks. For most of us, our concentration intensifies in the late morning. It drops off sharply straight after lunch, but there is normally another peak after the afternoon-tea break.

Organise the teaching programme around these peaks. Introduce new material or a difficult concept when mental activity is running high. Naturally there is some individual variation, but most people cannot concentrate hard for more than about 20 minutes at a time. If you must have lengthy sessions, break off periodically for a rest and, perhaps, a walk.

Arrange for periods of shared activity while mental activity is low. The experienced tutor often allows an extended lunchtime break during a tough programme or arranges a group discussion in which everybody is involved soon after the lunch break.

You can help people to keep alert by introducing an element of novelty into your programme — "I am going to spin this pen. When it stops, the person it points to will be asked to take the next session."

Experimenting

The experienced tutor will also experiment with different training techniques. When a plumber goes out on a job, he takes a kit full of different tools. You, too, should examine the job you will be undertaking and then select the most appropriate tools from your bagful of teaching techniques. When you have assessed a particular group, choose one of the 'tried and tested' teaching methods. If it is successful, build from there — if it fails, pick out a different method and try again.

Knowledge, Skills and Attitudes

The trainer will generally break down the course objectives into three main categories — knowledge, skills, and attitudes.

'Knowledge' can be transmitted in a lecture by using visual aids and hand-outs, but the development of a 'skill' requires repeated practice. Start from the stage your course members have reached, and build their skills and confidence gradually. Don't try to teach too much at the one time. Behavioural skills take time to develop. With a lifetime's accumulation of 'attitudes' in each of us, we cannot expect to change them very rapidly.

Selecting the Best Method

- **HAVE A CLEAR OBJECTIVE**
  What action do you want your course members to take after their course is finished?

  How will you know whether you have been successful?

- **TIME REQUIRED**
  Most trainers are too ambitious and they achieve very little. Allow plenty of time for adequate discussion and thinking.

- **CHOOSING YOUR ENVIRONMENT**
  If, for example, you intend to break the course into small groups, don't handicap them with a formal lecture theatre as the setting.

- **DOING YOUR HOMEWORK**
  It is important for you to learn as much as you can about your

students beforehand. If this proves too difficult, build in some early exercises which will help you to assess. For example, you might divide the group into pairs and ask the members of each pair to talk to one another about their hobbies and family and work experiences. Then ask each one in turn to report to the full group on what they have found out about their partner. (See Chapter 3, Section A — Planning).

■ PROVEN EXERCISES FIRST
Start with the exercises you feel confident will work. (Don't forget, however, to introduce new ways of teaching from time to time, in order to build up your 'kit' of teaching tools.) If, after experimenting, you find you have a failure on your hands, talk it out with the members themselves — as a group-learning experience. Never apologise for a failure, but do make sure you profit from the experience.

■ BEFORE YOU START CHOOSING
As a first step, the course should be broken down into a series of units or subjects. When you and the course members have agreed on a clear objective, it is a good idea to set them to work in small groups, on suggesting the topics they believe should be covered. The secret of success is to involve every member and to call upon their experience.

■ WHICH METHODS?
Having defined your subject area, your objectives, and the course contents, you should review the various teaching methods that are available and could be used.

For example, a supervision or management course could include:
— lectures
— case studies
— problem-solving exercises
— work exercises
— book and journal reviews
— small-group discussions
— group competitions
— role playing ('simulation exercises')
— introducing guests
— experience at chairing
— votes of thanks
— initiative exercises
— generating ideas ('brain storming') etc.
See Chapter 3, p. 31.

■ CHOOSE CAREFULLY
Whichever exercises you select, make sure they are related to the members' 'back home' situation. Never 'import' someone else's exercises, out of a 'foreign' book. Your students must see their training as relevant to their lives and important to their jobs.

- **PLAN FOR SOME 'CARRY-OVER'**
  Whenever possible you should help each member to draw up a detailed plan for personal action, to ensure the new behaviour patterns learned during the course will be put into practice 'back on the job'.

  But beware of starting a revolution. Quiet evolution is usually more acceptable and often achieves faster results. If their old social ties are resisting their new behaviour pattern, the whole course could prove to be just a waste of time and the members will be frustrated. In a formal organisation, acceptance of the course and full support of it by the top management are vital prerequisites. Get full support from top management before you start training.

- **ESTABLISH YOUR CREDENTIALS**
  Your first job must be to establish a rapport with your audience. Start with the exercises you like and with which you feel confident. Don't be in a hurry. Take your time, chat away, tell a few stories against yourself, and make sure that every member of the course becomes fully involved as soon as possible.

  The devices you use will depend upon
  — your experience,
  — your audience,
  — your environment,
  — your subject,
  — the time you have available, and
  — your objectives.

"There is nothing wrong with change if it's in the right direction."
Sir Winston Churchill

7 TRAINING TECHNIQUES

Many trainers and tutors spend too much time giving lectures which their students find irrelevant and boring. Participative training is usually more interesting, enjoyable and effective. It is always more challenging.

Add variety to your training by using some of the techniques listed below. The training methods are explained, their uses, advantages and limitations are discussed and hints are given for new trainers. They are listed in alphabetical order for ease of reference.

AUDIENCE-REACTION TEAM

A representative sample of three to five audience members are on stage with the speaker in order to clarify points which might not otherwise be understood. They ask questions of the speaker (or some resource person), either during or at the end of an address. A useful technique when an audience is very large or whenever it would be difficult to accept questions from the floor.

Uses

- Facilitates communication on a difficult subject.

- Provides audience feedback, enabling the speaker to gain a sample view of a large audience.

- Can lead a discussion at the end of an address and thus 'draw out' the speaker.

Advantages

- Easy to organise (but make sure the speaker is experienced enough to cope with such a team).

- Helps the expert who is not a good communicator to get the message across.

- Its presence may stimulate audience interest.

Limitations

- The speaker may object to a supposed inference that he/she is a poor communicator (or to being interrupted during the presentation).

- The audience's role is passive.

- Some team members may 'overparticipate' (show off), while others may be too timid for the job.

- Sometimes upsets a speaker.

Requirements

- Raised platform or stage, large enough for a speaker's rostrum, the chairman, and the team members.

- Every member of the audience should be able to see and hear each speaker.

Preparation and Procedure

- Organiser must discuss the technique fully with the guest speaker and gain approval to proceed.

- Chairman, guest speaker, and team meet together.

- Chairman introduces the topic to the full audience and describes the technique and the rules (also team's function and the reasons for using it).

- Chairman introduces the speaker (brief remarks on position held, experience, and any relevant special qualifications).

- Team reacts at the agreed-upon times.

Hints

- Select team members very carefully.

- Beware — unless your speaker is enthusiastic and confident, the team may cause undesirable tension.

'BUZZ' SESSION

A technique to involve a large audience directly in the discussion process by dividing up the members into small groups of five, six, or seven for a limited time (five to 15 minutes) to discuss a specific topic, with each member contributing to the discussion.

Uses

- To decide on questions for a speaker or panel.

- To decide on adequacy of available information.

- To plan future events.

- To produce recommendations.

- To evaluate a meeting or event.

Advantages

- Gives everyone a chance to participate without embarrassment.

- Gets people involved.

- Can become a source of fresh ideas.

- Competitive groups can provide a stimulating experience.

Limitations

- Individual participation is limited by time.

- Group contributions may be contradictory or difficult to reconcile.

- A skilled organiser is required.

- Difficult with large groups.

Requirements

- Easily movable chairs to facilitate quick organisation.

- If numbers permit, use open-formation seating (a circle or a 'U' arrangement is ideal because no one is hidden) — avoid theatre-type seating.

- Cards or papers for note taking (most people carry a pen).

Preparation and Procedure

- Calculate approximate number in audience.

- Work out the number of groups you will have (for example, an audience of 28 could provide four groups of seven).

- Having decided on four groups you would quickly 'number off' the audience, from one to four.

- Gather all the number 'ones' in one part of the room, the 'twos' in another part, and so on. ('Right. All the ''ones'' here please'.)

- Each group is instructed to select a leader and a recorder.

- The leader's job is to see that everyone has a chance to speak.

- The recorder summarises the discussion.

- At the end of the session, the leader or the recorder of each group reports orally to the full meeting.

- The organiser and an assistant collect and summarise all the reports and process them.

Hints

- Time is saved by the organiser nominating the leaders and the recorders.

- A good technique to gather additional information for a resource speaker and for setting up questions.

- Set up the groups before the lecture and ask each one to carry out 'selective listening', for example:

    - Group 1 — note points that require further amplification.
    - Group 2 — look for omissions on which you would like the speaker's view.
    - Group 3 — list points with which you disagree.

- Can be used to get more out of a technical film by providing it with greater purpose.

CASE STUDY

Comprehensive oral, written, and/or filmed account of an event or series of related events.

Uses

- Presents a situation problem for discussion.

- Problem-solving technique.

- Teaching problem-solving processes.

- Builds up a complete picture.

Advantages

- Provides relevant detail.

- Helps to identify alternative solutions.

- Helps to develop analytical, problem-solving skills.

Limitations

- Can be time consuming.

- Relevance may not always be obvious.

- Stimulates some people, but irritates others.

Requirements

They will vary with the type of case — a stage or some other, fully visible area will be needed if you are going to 'act out' a problem; a film calls for a blackout and for a suitable screen and projector (check on their availability well beforehand).

Procedure

- Chairman introduces the topic and explains the case study and what is required.

- Chairman guides the discussion toward achieving the desired result.

Hints

- Allow plenty of time before the start for members to study a written case.

- Can be very effective if small groups compete in seeking solutions.

- A debate on possible solutions can be worthwhile when a capable chairman is available to keep the speakers 'on course'.

- Some 'red herrings' are desirable in any case study, but take care not to build in too many at the expense of getting the main message across.

- Don't waste time in looking for a scapegoat.

- The best case studies are built upon actual problems (but take care to hide the identity of the people involved).

- A common technique in management courses is to ask each member to describe an office problem as a case study for group solution, and later reveal (and sometimes discuss) how it was in fact handled.

COMMITTEE

Small group selected to act on behalf of the entire group or organisation. May function as an 'executive' committee or 'house' committee, and may be further broken down into subcommittees or 'task forces'.

Uses

- Represents an organisation between its annual meetings.

- To plan, promote, and organise a special event, such as a seminar or convention.

- As an advisory group.

- To study a particular problem and to come up with recommendations for solving it.

- Evaluating a particular occasion.

Advantages

- Makes use of people with experience and the time to carry out specialist assignments.

- Utilises a variety of different interests and experiences.

- Provides a good training ground for future leaders.

Limitations

- Difficulty of appointing a compatible team.

- Often difficult to find enough people with the necessary time and capable of assuming the responsibility.

- Must act on behalf of whole organisation and needs its support, which sometimes is not given.

Requirements

- An environment which will promote communication.

- Facilities for reaching and recording decisions.

Procedure

- Normally 'democratically' elected by whole organisation, but can be appointed by the president or other elected officers (especially applies to subcommittees, working parties, or task forces).

- Should be given a set of rules or guidelines (in large organisations they form a 'constitution').

- Often required to carry out a particular assignment and to report back to the whole organisation or its representatives.

- Such a committee is then given further instructions or is dissolved.

Hints

- A committee's instructions should always be clear — what is expected and when.

- A committee usually needs a chairman to lead it, and a secretary to record its findings, decisions, and recommendations, and to organise the venue and time of its meetings.

- A committee that is faced with a formidable task can be broken up into subcommittees in which selected members are given areas of responsibility and the power to co-opt their own working parties.

- Committee work should enable the less experienced person to work alongside and to profit from the expertise of the more experienced.

CONFERENCE

Large or small group of people with common interests, meeting together by common consent.

Uses

- A group with a common interest discusses a narrow technical area ('Dairy Farmers' Conference' or 'Overseas Aid Conference').

- To develop promotion plans ('Save Our Native Forests' Conference).

Advantages

- Members usually discuss topics of high interest to them.

- Members are usually voluntary attenders.

- Enthusiasts are brought together to share their expertise and to plan.

Limitations

- Often hard to predict number who will attend.

- Arrangements must often be made to provide for guest speakers, a venue, catering, accommodation, and various other costs for an unknown number.

- Degree of success is often hard to measure.

Requirements

- Auditorium, comfortable seating, small meeting rooms, catering, toilets, transport arrangements, accommodation, special equipment for the media and for speakers, audio-visual aids, display facilities (notice boards and suchlike).

- Promotion and prepublicity, registrations, compiling and publishing programme, handouts, and post publicity.

- Accurate evaluating and follow-up procedures.

Hints

- People need to be told 'What's in it for me?' — a clear objective is needed.

- Decide on those you wish to invite. Find out their background and the extent of their information.

- Early programme planning is desirable. (The best way to finalise speakers is to visit them or tell them by telephone what the conference is all about, what is expected from them, and who will be attending.) Details should then be sent to the speakers.

- A wide range of publicity is desirable.

- Look after your guest speakers well — delegate someone to look after and to fuss over each one of them, and don't forget a follow-up 'thank you' letter.

- Post-conference publicity is just as important as prepublicity — try and get messsages to the people who were unable to attend.

- 'Balance the books' and pay the bills as soon after the conference as possible.

CONVENTION

An assembly of representatives of the regional groups of a parent organisation.

Uses

- Educational (guest speakers, forums, workshops, and so on).

- To plan policies, objectives, and strengthening strategies.

- To elect officers or candidates.

- As a training ground.

- For any combination of these uses.

Advantages

- An educational experience for individuals from a wide geographic area.

- Can produce a consensus from the many local groups that may make up an organisation.

- Provides the individual with a chance to get to know the organisation and to see it in action.

■ Helps to share experiences and to make contacts.

■ Helps to guide and train new appointees to local positions.

Limitations

■ Considerable work on advance planning and promotion is required.

■ Can be costly.

■ Needs an environment that is ideal for large numbers.

■ The individual can be made to feel insignificant.

■ A group whose ideas or remits are rejected may be resentful.

Requirements

■ For the general sessions, a large auditorium in which everybody can see and hear in comfort.

■ A number of small meeting rooms.

■ Support services — production and audio-visual.

■ Adequate sleeping accommodation.

■ Catering facilities, toilets, and suchlike.

■ Transport.

Preparation and Procedure

■ Plan on a national scale.

■ Set up sufficient local working parties.

■ Carefully plan arrangements for adequate facilities.

■ Draw up and publish programme details advising key members as soon as possible.

■ Advertise.

■ Appoint and brief the chairman.

■ Opening session with a 'keynote' address.

■ Summary, educational, and business sessions.

■ 'Cocktail' sessions and/or a formal dinner.

- Final summary sessions (reviewing and so on).

- Such evaluating and 'follow-up' as is needed.

Hints

- The organiser is to co-ordinate the planning and see that it is implemented on time (check and double check this) — not to do the actual work.

- Local working parties must be involved at an early stage in the planning.

- The organiser should delegate areas of responsibility to reliable people, who should be given the power to co-opt their own working parties.

- Good communications are necessary from the very start of the planning.

- Guest speakers and 'draw cards' need to be 'signed up' and briefed early.

DEBATE

A formal contest in which participants present opposing views on a controversial topic. This can take the form of an argument between two people but in most formal debates there are two teams, each with three members.

(A formal debate is a good participative training method involving many people as debaters, chairperson, timekeeper, judges and often commentators from the audience.)

Uses

- To examine a subject in depth and work out arguments 'for' and 'against' a given point of view.

- To show how essential it is to research a subject thoroughly.

- To make participants think logically.

- To help participants think and speak concisely.

- To develop team spirit among the participants.

Advantages

- An active learning experience involving many people.

- Often more interesting than a lecture.

- Useful in changing attitudes.

- Teaches participants to think rapidly in front of an audience and to cope with interjections.

Limitations

- Time consuming. A great deal of research and preparation must be done before the debate if it is to be successful.

- Must be run as a formal event with chairperson, judges and audience.

- Some participants may be too self-conscious or timid to debate successfully.

Requirements

- Six people who are enthusiastic and prepared to speak on a given topic, i.e. two teams of three members.

- An interesting, controversial subject with wide audience appeal. The topic should be stated clearly and affirmatively e.g. 'That A should be B' NOT 'That A should not be B.' The affirmative team must then debate that the statement is correct, while the negative team must deny or contradict, trying to prove that the statement is false.

- Access to a library for research on the topic.

- A skilled chairperson or moderator.

- Competent judges.

- An audience.

- A set of rules familiar to both teams.

- A timekeeper with stop-watch, bell or warning lights.

- A suitable venue, preferably with a stage or raised platform with seating for seven people.

Preparation and Procedure

- The chairperson or moderator has complete control of the meeting and sits between the teams. The affirmative team sits at the chairperson's right.

- The chairperson reads the rules of debate to the teams and audience.

- The chairperson is responsible for the times allowed for speakers, but may appoint a time keeper.

- The usual time allowed is ten minutes for the leaders' opening speeches and eight minutes for all subsequent speeches.

- Order of Debate
  1. Leader of affirmative team.
  2. Leader of negative team.
  3. Second speaker — affirmative.
  4. Second speaker — negative.
  5. Third speaker — affirmative.
  6. Third speaker — negative.
  7. Concluding address by leader of negative team, summarising their arguments. No fresh material should be introduced at this stage.
  8. Closing address by leader of affirmative team.

- Speakers should address the chairperson, but face the audience.

- The leaders should define the subject clearly and concisely.

- The timekeeper should give a warning one minute before the allocated time and again at the final time. Speakers are usually penalised if they exceed their times.

- Speakers who consider they have been misrepresented, or a leader who considers new arguments are being introduced in an opponent's concluding address, may rise to a point of order. The chairperson must give a ruling immediately.

- The timekeeper can extend a speaker's time to compensate for the time taken up by a point of order.

- Members of the opposing team can interject during a speech if the interjections are concise and relevant.

- Judges usually allocate points or marks for:
  definition of the subject
  subject matter
  eloquence
  deportment
  criticism
  summary and conclusion

- If teams score equal marks, the team whose leader scores the most points in the closing address is judged the winner.

Hints

■ Make training fun by selecting humorous topics and witty speakers.

■ Select topics carefully. A good topic should give both teams an equal chance of winning.

■ Speakers should be advised to:
1. Clarify the subject
2. State arguments clearly. Back them up with evidence and illustrate them with ancedotes.
3. Restate the arguments briefly.

■ Don't waste time while the judges are totalling their marks and preparing comments on performances. Encourage audience participation by asking them for comments or getting them to indicate which team they thought was the winner by a show of hands.

DEMONSTRATION

The performance of an action (or the explanation of a procedure) before an audience, to enable the viewers to perform the same action (under guidance, if necessary).

Uses

■ To teach a particular task.

■ To introduce a new procedure or technique.

■ To reinforce a point.

■ To introduce a new product.

■ To illustrate or dramatise some point in a training programme.

Advantages

■ What is seen is more likely to be believed and remembered than what is heard or read.

■ Trying for oneself is a powerful aid to learning.

■ The pace can be flexible and the action can be repeated as often as necessary.

■ Can utilise the 'real thing' or a model of it.

Limitations

- More suitable for small groups.

- Can be expensive and time consuming.

- Can raise transport and setting-up problems.

- Special conditions (such as a raised platform) are often required.

Requirements

- The provision of adequate facilities is most important. Everybody must be able to see and to practise with the demonstration equipment. Power points, good lighting, and a raised platform may be other essentials. For a large-scale demonstration, a barrier may be required to keep people from crowding and to allow more people a view.

Preparation and Procedure

- Collect the necessary materials and equipment and select a suitable site.

- Practise techniques beforehand.

- Explain purpose and objective, then carry out demonstration.

- Invite audience to practise the techniques under guidance.

- Volunteers are tested to see whether they have acquired the demonstrated skill.

Hints

- To demonstrate effectively, you must be familiar with your equipment and skilled in using it.

- Make sure the audience fully appreciates the purpose of your demonstration — a visual aid can be used to reinforce your words.

- The easiest way to a successful demonstration is to build on individual experiences.

- Students practise best in their own time, without too many observers — some get very nervous while others are watching and criticising.

- Practice, practice, and more practice is the rule for mastering a complicated procedure.

DISCUSSION GROUP

Two or more persons who come together to talk informally and to deliberate on a topic of mutual concern — experiences are shared, opinions expressed, alternatives discussed, and action is planned — interaction between individual members or between similar groups may provide the catalyst for problem solving and for effective planning.

Uses

- To identify, explore, and seek out solutions to problems.

- To develop plans for action.

- Where necessary, to change attitudes through an amicable examination of the evidence.

- To develop leadership skills.

- As a supplementary technique in many types of training.

Advantages

- Such a group pools experiences, abilities, and knowledge in order to reach recognised goals.

- Should provide for the full participation of every member.

- Can establish a democratic consensus.

- Can stimulate a desire to learn and to share.

Limitations

- Can be time consuming, particularly if persons with strong convictions or widely different backgrounds are involved.

- Preliminary exercises are needed before serious group activity is possible.

Requirements

- See Chapter 5 — Participative Training.

EXERCISE

A work assignment, designed to provide practice in a skill or technique — useful to review skills already learnt and as a basis for self-instructional learning.

Uses

- To demonstrate a skill or technique.

- To provide practice.

- To reinforce or to test learning.

- To test initiative.

- To review already acquired skills.

Advantages

- Can promote familiarity with the real thing.

- Helps to build confidence or independence.

- Represents self-instructional learning.

- Can be used to provide a welcome break.

- Can help to develop initiative.

Limitations

- Worthwhile only when well planned and tested.

- Often requires a good deal of organising.

- The degree of skill that is acquired must depend upon the individual capabilities.

Requirements

- They depend on the type of exercise. An adequate work space and tools; a carefully planned appointment schedule; adequate travel and accommodation arrangements; and up-to-date maps may all be necessary.

Hints

- During a lengthy workshop, field exercises can provide a worthwhile break for both tutors and participants.

- Every exercise needs to be both challenging and relevant. For example, 'Go and investigate the situation and prepare a report to the director. Produce your recommendations by [mention date]'.

- The students must always be given clear instructions on what is expected of them and by when.

- A critical but helpful feedback is an essential part of any worthwhile exercise—and don't forget to praise.

EXHIBIT

Display of visual information — can comprise models, photographs, visuals, and/or the 'real thing', with varying amounts of detail.

Uses

- To reinforce a lecture.

- As information for a conference or a convention.

- As a training 'tool' — students examine at their leisure the details, photographs, books, or whatever else is included.

Advantages

- Can be used a number of times.

- Can be adapted and updated to meet varying needs.

- Can be used to encourage participation, so that each individual learns at the most convenient time and at his/her own speed.

- Can involve hearing, touch, taste, and/or smell as well as sight.

Limitations

- Can be costly.

- Difficult to use effectively with a large group.

- Needs ample space and a suitable, well-lit environment.

- May be expensive to pack and to transport.

Hints

- Make sure your exhibit is designed and arranged for clear visibility.

- Keep the message simple and clear — most exhibits are overcrowded, with too much writing.

- Four basic rules for a successful exhibit are:
  1. First catch your audience's attention with a gimmick.
  2. Try to get each member involved.
  3. Tell them your message.
  4. To those who show interest, give a handout with further details, including where to go for more information.

- Every exhibit should look fresh and interesting.

- An active exhibit with living things moving or machines at work, or with a tape-slide or video demonstration, will attract most attention.

FILM

Audio-visual, often detailed presentation of a subject, directed by one or more experts.

Uses

- To present factual material in a direct, logical manner.

- To provide a break in a training programme.

- To show things not readily accessible to the individual viewer or the naked eye.

- To give a time sequence (seasons, for example).

- To arouse or increase interest.

- To illustrate various points of view.

Advantages

- Tells exactly the same story each time it is shown.

- Suitable for a wide range of subjects.

- Can easily be repeated.

- Its running time is known (or is easily discoverable).

Limitations

- Is costly to make or to buy.

- It can be difficult to find a film on a suitable topic at the right level for your particular audience.

- The film producer takes over control of your audience.

- No one can talk back to a film — it's one-way communication.

- Some trainers rely too heavily on the film.

- Requires expensive equipment and a degree of expertise.

Requirements

- Apart from the film(s), a projector that works and a screen are essential.

- A darkened room for showing.

- A qualified operator.

- A power source.

- Everybody must be able to see and to hear.

Preparation and Procedure

- Set up and check the equipment in a room that can be darkened at the appropriate time (sun shining on a curtain can interfere with a blackout).

- Thread the projector and run the film through beforehand to make sure there are no breaks and that you can work the machine; also, to get the sound levels right (but remember that the acoustics of a full room necessitate more volume than an empty room).

- Be sure to rewind and rethread the film so that it is ready for showing.

- Rewind the film after the final showing, before you return it to its canister.

Hints

- Wind the power cord around the leg of the table so that any late arrivers who trip on the cord in the dark don't pull the projector on to the floor.

- Arouse audience interest in the film by individual and group assignments.

- Test the audience after the showing to see how much has been learnt — a re-run may be worthwhile.

- Select carefully the time you show a film — not right after a heavy meal, for example.

FORUM

A public assembly in which everyone is given a chance to voice his/her views.

Uses

- Can be an orderly discussion after a topic has been introduced by a speaker, a panel, or a film, or in some similar way.

- Can help to gauge public opinion on a controversial issue (the introduction of new legislation, for example).

Advantages

- Allows audience members to participate (even in a large meeting).

- Helps to develop a group opinion by testing ideas.

- Can also contribute to the idea development that must precede group action.

Limitations

- Its success depends upon the ability of the chairman and the attitude of the audience.

- Heated debates may be stimulating but can delay the arrival at a consensus.

- Can get out of control when the topic is controversial and pressure groups get organised.

- Expert acoustic advice and equipment are necessary for large meetings.

Requirements

- An adequate hall or auditorium is necessary, depending on the numbers.

- Every member of the audience must be able to hear the speaker — at a large meeting, therefore, the speakers must come to a microphone or be within range of a 'gun' microphone or a transmitting microphone.

- A capable chairman and (if necessary) assistants.

Procedure

- One or more speakers introduce and develop the subject.

- The chairman calls for questions or comments from the audience.

- The chairman immediately repeats each question asked from the floor and directs it to the appropriate authority.

- The chairman maintains control and sees that all the comments from the 'floor' are relevant and brief — it is a good idea to summarise the arguments from time to time.

- The final summary, leading up to the conclusions that were reached, is also best done by the chairman or by a selected reporter.

Hints

- The chairman must be seen to be fair in maintaining control and must have a good sense of humour.

- It is wise to insist on 'One question at a time please, and keep your comments brief'. (The comments and the questions very easily get mixed up).

- Assistants who are stationed in strategic locations in the audience can help to identify the people who want to speak and can hold the transmitting microphones.

- Questions and comments are most easily recorded (for 'proceedings') by reporters summarising them into portable tape recorders — few people can ask a clear question and few speakers can give an exact answer.

- When the audience is very large you should call for 'clearly printed' questions — and have a large tin or box on the front of the stage or in the foyer to receive them.

GENERATING IDEAS ('BRAIN-STORMING')

The unrestrained offering of ideas by all members of a group where members put forward every conceivable idea (practicable and impracticable) on a subject.

'Let me ask you how many seeds there are in this apple I'm holding. Let's count them. There are eight. Now let me ask you how many potential apples there are in any one of these apple seeds. We've no way of counting that. The same is true of our group. We may know how many people are in our group, but the total of their ideas is difficult to determine.' 'Brain-storming' is a technique for estimating this.

Uses

- As a pre-evaluation discussion, to produce as many new ideas as possible — quantity before quality.

- To encourage practical minds to think 'quantitatively', beyond day-to-day problems, rather than 'qualitatively'.

- To make progress on a problem when the more conventional techniques have failed.

- To develop creative thinking.

Advantages

- Often produces a solution to a previously insoluble problem.

- Many people are encouraged by the freedom of expression offered by this technique.

- Everybody can contribute and participate.

Limitations

- Many people have difficulty in getting started, away from practicalities.

- Many of the suggestions that are made may be worthless.

- In setting priorities in the evaluation session, other people's ideas must be criticised (but make sure it is done constructively).

Requirements

- Comfortable, distraction-free environment.

- An enthusiastic, skilful leader.

- One or more recorders — to write up (on a chalkboard, an overhead projector, or a large paper pad) the ideas that are generated.

- Where possible, a semicircular, sitting or standing arrangement.

Preparation and Procedure

- The leader plays the important role of 'catalyst' explaining the rules and stimulating the group members. A good warming-up exercise is to produce some common object such as a brick, and to ask each person to write down a list of all possible uses for it. Arrange a competition. After a set time (say 10 minutes) find out who has the longest list and ask its compiler to read it out. Then call for any ideas that have not already been mentioned. Repeat the exercise with a variety of objects, until every member can produce a flow of ideas on any subject. By then, the group will have been warmed up for a 'real' situation.

- The leader should explain the procedure and the recorders should be selected and briefed.

- As the ideas are called out, they are written down for everyone to see.
  - The greater their number, the better the chance of coming up with a solution.
  - Don't allow interruptions or criticism, but look for ways to combine or improve ideas.
  - 'Free wheeling', wild ideas are to be encouraged — it is easier to 'tone down' than to think up ideas.

- Take a break as soon as the enthusiasm starts to fail.

- Examine each idea — does it have any practical application for our problem?

- Encourage each group member to pick out the 'best' solution then compare and discuss the suggestions.

Hints

- Set deadlines — once your group is responding, work 'under pressure' for limited periods only (not more than 45 minutes, but preferably less).

- If the group cannot 'get started', take a short break and start again.

- Group work should arouse friendly rivalry and stimulate the flow of ideas — advance notice of the discussion topic should get people thinking about it beforehand, perhaps overnight.

- A group that starts to 'go stale' or some of whose members are inhibited should be broken up and sent off for a limited time to discuss the topic in pairs.

- Keep the groups small — up to eight members, including the leader and the recorders.

- Encourage small groups to compete for the 'best' solution (competition is a great stimulus).

Five-step Problem Solver

1. Define — make sure each member understands and agrees on the nature of the problem.

2. List its causes — encourage 'lateral' thinking.

3. 'Brain-storm' for possible solutions.

4. Choose the best suggestion — discuss and, if necessary, discard, examining every idea for an immediate or future application.

5. Plan the action (how to implement the chosen suggestion).

INTERVIEW

Meeting of two or more people face to face, usually for the purpose of questioning and examining one of them.

Uses

- To explore a topic in some depth.

- Can provide an informal approach.

- Can be a good way to handle a controversial issue.

Advantages

- Less formal than a lecture.

- Can be made more interesting than a lecture.

- The audience is represented by the interviewer(s).

Limitations

- The audience's role is passive.

- The interviewer must be skilled and must have done his/her homework.

- Talking to an interviewer in front of an audience can be daunting.

- Needs people who can relate well (and with, preferably, a sense of humour).

Requirements

- Comfortable seating.

- Good acoustics — everybody must be able to see and to hear.

- A stage large enough to hold protagonists, microphones, and amplifying equipment.

Preparation and Procedure

- A meeting between the interviewer and an appropriate 'expert' is arranged — ground rules, topics, line of questioning, and physical requirements (taking account of type and size of audience) are set.

- Set up the hall (stage, seating, lighting, and sound system).

- When the time arrives, the chairman introduces the topic, the 'expert', and the interviewer.

- The interviewer asks questions designed to explore and to develop the topic.

- Questions from the audience may be taken at the end.

- The chairman sums up the discussion (perhaps calling for the vote of thanks from the audience).

Hints

- The style of the interview is determined by the knowledge and the personaiity of the 'performers' — a relaxed, informally 'probing' interview is best.

- The interviewer must select each question carefully — repeating it in a slightly different form will help to make sure that each member of the audience has heard it.

- As well as putting the carefully prepared questions, the interviewer needs to be able to improvise apposite questions as the occasion arises.

- The expert should be set at ease before the interviewer moves on to the more difficult questions.

- The interviewer who has the ability to do so can also act as chairman.

LECTURE (SPEECH)

A usually carefully prepared, rather formal dissertation by one with claims to be an expert on the particular theme.

Uses

- To present factual material in a logical sequence.

- To present one or more points of view on a controversial subject.

- To recount personal experiences.

- To entertain or to arouse an audience.

- To call for action.

- To stimulate thought, thus opening up a subject for discussion and further study.

Advantages

- Suitable for an audience of any size.

- Easy to organise.

- Some people learn more easily listening than reading.

- Simple recall exercises make its effectiveness easy to assess.

Limitations

- The audience's role is passive.

- There is a one-way flow of information.

- Efficient listening demands concentration.

- The lecture is the traditional, but very ineffective, method of imparting skills.

- Audience feedback is limited.

- The expert is not always a good speaker.

- Good speakers can be hard to find.

Requirements

- Speaker must be visible to, and heard by, the chairman and every member of the audience.

- Stage or raised platform (speakers' rostrum) with microphone, amplifiers, and loudspeakers when size of audience requires them.

- Visual aids (projector and screen) when called for by speaker.

Procedure

- The chairman introduces the speaker, with a brief statement of his/her qualifications and expertise in the selected topic.

- The chairman should ensure the speaker is given a fair hearing, in the best possible conditions.

- At the end of the speech, the chairman (with the speaker's prior consent) should call for questions or points for discussion.

- Finally, the chairman should call upon a member of the audience to make a brief speech of thanks to the speaker.

Hints

- The effectiveness of a speech can be improved by encouraging the audience to take notes.

- Use visual aids as lecturer's 'signposts' or memory joggers — remember, 'a good picture is worth a thousand words'.

- Make good use of stories and anecdotes and other figures of speech to illustrate your points.

- Introduce devices such as repetition to heighten drama.

- Review and summarise regularly. 'Tell them what you are going to tell them, tell it to them, then tell them what you have just told them'.

- Be careful not to cram too many points in a single lecture.

- Give out copies summarising your speech at its conclusion.

- Prepare your audience for selective listening. 'We will try to find out tomorrow how much you have learnt today'.

LISTENING TEAM

Its members listen to the speakers, take notes, and question or summarise at the close (unlike the reaction team, they do not interrupt), thus providing interaction between the speaker(s) and a large audience.

Uses

- To take notes and to question a formal speaker or the symposium participants.

- To listen to, evaluate, and question a speaker (or group of speakers) in formal or informal discussions.

Advantages

- The audience is 'represented' in a formal way.

- The team identifies and clarifies the issues, questions and opinions developed by the speaker(s).

- A summary at the end will aid audience recall and help to avoid confusion.

Limitations

- When the team is being selected, the views of the majority of the audience need to be kept in mind.

- Each member needs to be knowledgeable on the subject, and should have no known biases.

Requirements

- Sufficient comfortable seats, arranged so that everybody in the audience can hear and see the speakers and the listening team.

- A stage or platform large enough for everybody who needs to be on it.

- Seats, a table, and lighting for the listening team.

- Microphones and an amplifying system powerful enough to allow the speaker(s) to be heard by everybody.

Preparation and Procedure

- Inform the speaker(s) beforehand about the team.

- Select the team, instruct it on its role, and introduce it to the speaker(s), with whom it should spend some time informally, getting acquainted.

- The audience is told of the team and its function is explained.

- During the speech(es) the team members take notes and prepare questions and summaries.

- The team reports.

- The chairman sums up.

Hints

- Be sure to gain the prior approval of the speaker(s) to the use of this technique.

- Take care in selecting the team not to pick any member with a political axe to grind.

- Make sure you brief each party well, so that everybody knows precisely what is required of them.

MULTI-MEDIA PACKAGE

A packaged set of teaching materials on a specific topic, designed for self-teaching — usually consists of filmstrips or slides or a tape-slide presentation, a programmed workbook, discussion questions, and reference material.

Uses

- Adaptable to any technical subject.

- Suitable for most self-learning situations.

- Suitable also for automated group learning.

Advantages

- Does not require a tutor.

- Materials are carefully selected, and the package is specifically designed and carefully tested.

- Learning is precise and degree of accomplishment can be measured.

Limitations

- It is inflexible.

- It is expensive to prepare.

- Its packaging and postage can be expensive.

Requirements

- Audio-visual equipment to produce it.

- A suitable package to contain it.

- A quiet room for studying it.

Procedure

- The learning package is divided up into modules.

  — Read the instructions.

  — Run through the tape/slide module.

  — Read the references.

  — Work through the workbook module.

  — Listen to second tape module or view its slides.

- Afterwards it is useful for the learners to come together in small groups in order to answer questions or to discuss problems or questions that are raised.

- Finally, the answers should be checked and the slides and references viewed again.

Hints

- Use this technique to bring busy professional people up to date with specific technical literature.

- The packages don't have to be expensive or complicated — start with a box file, photocopy the current literature, add a set of slides, prepare a work plan and apposite questions, add a voice tape from an authority on the subject, and you are 'in business'.

- The technique works best when the individual is allowed to proceed at his/her own pace and afterwards take part in a small discussion group to share experiences.

PANEL

A group of (usually) three to five specially knowledgeable persons, in full view of an audience, holding an orderly conversation on a set topic. (Differs from a symposium in that, after sometimes making a short, formal statement, the panel members talk only to one another.)

Uses

- To identify and explore a topic, issue, or problem.

- To weigh up the pros and cons of a course of action.

- To assist the audience to understand a complex issue.

Advantages

- Frequent changes of speaker and viewpoint should maintain a high interest level.

- Can be very relaxed and informal and thus establish a favourable audience reaction.

- If you select the panel members carefully, all sides of an argument can be presented.

Limitations

- A skilled chairman is essential.

- Panel members need to be selected for balance and for their ability to communicate — any extreme differences of opinion may block progress toward a solution.

- The subject is not necessarily considered in the logical order.

Requirements

- Each speaker must be audible and visible to every member of the audience.

- A good stage setting, together with adequate microphones (if need be) and a satisfactory sound system.

Preparation and Procedure

- Organiser sets a clear objective.

- Panel members are selected and briefed.

- Meeting is held to discuss the objective and the 'ground rules'.

- Programme and publicity are printed and distributed.

- The stage is set, the sound system is tested, and sufficient seats are set out.

- Audience assembles and chairman briefly introduces the topic and the panel (stating their qualifications).

- Each panel member may make a brief formal statement (usually five to 10 minutes) setting out his/her point of view before the exchange of ideas and comments.

- May be followed by a forum to broaden the discussion and to involve the audience. (Agreement to this needs to be obtained beforehand from the panel members).

Hints

- Take care in selecting your chairman and the panel members — the extrovert and the good communicator are needed.

- It is a good idea to explain the 'ground rules' to the audience beforehand.

- The good chairman presents a balanced picture and makes sure that each member of the panel becomes involved — that the questions are shared about.

- The group chairman will try to relax the panel members and to maintain a sense of humour.

- On many such occasions a summary by the chairman or the tutor is a good way to conclude the discussion.

- Don't forget to arrange for a vote of thanks from the floor to the chairman and the panel — and for formal 'thank you' letters to everybody after the event.

PEER TEACHING
('Peer-assisted learning' or 'Peer mediated instruction')

Small groups of peers act as both teacher and learner by switching roles (differs from peer tutoring, in which a student who is gifted in a subject helps another who is having difficulty in it).

Uses

- To break up a large class into small 'learning cells'.

- To reduce anxiety levels at the start of a training course by involving the whole class in an active learning process.

- To explore some particular subject in greater depth than the rest.

Advantages

- A 'one-to-one' situation.

- Provides an active learning system for large 'lecture' classes.

- Reduces student feelings of isolation and boredom.

- Gives the students greater responsibility in their own learning.

- Provides an immediate feedback (for self-evaluating).

Limitations

- Peers are seldom experts in a subject and are not trained teachers.

- They are easily sidetracked by being asked irrelevant questions.

- The class as a whole may have difficulty in concentrating because of the noise being made by the groups.

- The student may feel antipathy toward his/her partner or at the idea of what is a highly structured method of studying.

- Progress can be impeded if competition among the groups becomes too strong.

Requirements

- Ample space.

- A quiet, sound-proof room.

Procedure

- Brief the class on the technique and its requirements.

- Break up the class into pairs or groups of three ('triads').

- Each student must be called upon to gain experience in both the teaching and the learning roles — each member of every group shares in asking the questions on a common reading assignment or on some other prepared assignment or set topic.

- The tutor is always available to supervise, to help solve problems or settle arguments, and to advise when necessary.

- The tutor should run a concluding session for the full class, to attempt to answer any questions that came to light in the learning 'cells'.

Hints

- Peer teaching can be a valuable technique and is well worth trying in a variety of situations.

- Most of the people in a large group are usually sitting next to friends. This tends to make peer teaching easier to get started than it might otherwise be.

- If the room is inadequate, send the class outside for half an hour to walk or sit in pairs, working on the planned assignment (perhaps over a cup of coffee).

- After paired discussion on a topic, any knowledge gaps should have become apparent — they should form the basis of questions to one of the resource speakers.

PROGRAMMED INSTRUCTION

Material presented in any one or more of a variety of ways (texts, tape-slides, multi-media, or a teaching machine or computer) as a series of small, carefully graduated, sequential steps, the mastering of which requires the active participation of the learner at his/her own preferred pace ('self-paced learning').

Uses

- For learning at a distance, by correspondence (particularly adults, in their own home).

- Ideal for in-service training — where students come to a central training unit in their own time to work on a learning unit.

- As a break from more-formal training.

Advantages

- Is as effective as conventional methods, and sometimes faster.

- Students do their own marking.

- Self testing produces immediate feedback.

- Students themselves identify areas that require further study.

- In step-by-step study, the learner acts as his/her own pace setter.

Limitations

- Developing and pretesting of programmes can be costly in both time and money.

- There is a shortage of programmed-learning material.

- Too many students will lead to competition for the machines (computer, tape-slide machine, and so on).

- Most students tend to prefer more-sociable learning systems.

- The inflexibility of what is a highly structured method.

Requirement

- The student must have a private 'quiet area' — in his/her accommodation or in the training area.

Procedure

- A learning 'package' is divided up into units or modules.

- The student is required to follow instructions that are based on the media being used.

- Reinforcing exercises are set.

- Each set of work is marked before the student is allowed to proceed.

Hints

- The most effective learning occurs from challenging, stimulating, encouraging exercises — variety is the key to teaching and to learning.

- Programmed learning can be boring, or it can be 'fun' — make sure it is also challenging.

- Programmed learning can be very encouraging for slow learners.

- Don't make the learning units too small — students will grow bored.

- If possible, make the learning machines available outside 'working hours', to encourage their use.

QUESTION TIME

An organised session that follows formal speeches or a forum or panel — members of the audience are invited to submit to the speakers any questions they may have.

Uses

- To clarify points made during the more formal sessions.

- To amplify points that were not fully covered.

- To seek new information.

- To involve the audience more closely.

Advantages

- Provides feedback to the speaker(s).

- Stimulates greater audience interest in the topic.

- Encourages more-careful listening.

- It is psychologically sound for audience members to know they are able to participate, but do not have to do so.

Limitations

- At the close of a long session the audience may be weary.

- Time usually limits the number of questions.

- Physically difficult to handle in a large audience.

- Can be 'taken over' by a few vocal members.

- Most members are too shy to participate.

Requirement

- Every member of the audience must be able to see and to hear the questioners and to hear the answers.

Procedure

- The chairman sets the ground rules: 'One question at a time, please, and keep your questions short and to the point'.

- The chairman should repeat each question that is asked so that everybody can hear it (and to give the speaker time to sort out a reply).

- The chairman should also identify each questioner (by name, if possible) and 'ration out' the time that is available.

- Finally, it is the chairman who keeps control, comments when necessary, sums up, and keeps the meeting running to time.

Hints

- The success of such an exercise depends largely on the experience and ability of the chairman — not only in keeping the audience under control and in good humour, but also in seeing that the answers given by the speaker(s) are to the point and as complete as possible.

- In a large audience, transmitting or gun microphones may be needed (the chairman may have 'spotters' in the audience to assist him/her, or the questioners can be asked beforehand to come up to a centrally placed microphone).

- Audience members can be asked to hand in written questions during breaks — but make sure they are printed questions so the chairman can read them easily.

- If a large number of questions is received, a preliminary sorting should ensure that only the more appropriate ones are used.

- One or more boxes or tins can be placed in the foyer to receive the written questions.

- If insufficient questions are forthcoming, call for a five-minute break and ask each audience member to combine with his/her neighbour in thinking up a question — that method usually works.

ROLE PLAYING AND DRAMA SPOTS

A 'real-life' situation (but with no script and no set dialogue) is improvised and acted out in front of the group, which then discusses the implications of the performance for the situation under consideration.

Uses

- To examine a problem in human relationships — for example, an extension worker or a social worker who is required to deal with a 'difficult' client.

- To seek out possible solutions to an emotion-laden problem.

- To provide a group with insight into attitudes that differ sharply from their own.

- To practise new skills.

Advantages

- An effective way of stimulating discussion that is aimed at problem solving.

- Gives the actor a chance to assume the personality of (to think and act like) another human being, which should lead to a better understanding of the other person's point of view.

- Can be an effective means of avoiding the real-life dangers of the 'trial-and-error' approach.

- Can add variety, drama, and fun to a formal training programme.

- The actors are sometimes able to explain cultural differences simply and clearly.

Limitations

- Some people are too timid or self-conscious to act a role successfully.

- Role playing loses some of its effect when the audience is too large.

Requirements

- Each member of the audience must be able to see the action.

- Actors seem to prefer being against a wall or on a stage, away from their audience.

Procedure

- The group leader must clearly define the situation ('set the scene') before the role playing begins.

- Role playing can be introduced without any warning, but it is better to give the actors a little time to get used to the idea — they will then sometimes produce a very polished performance.

- The tutor should set a time limit beforehand: 'You have 10 minutes in which to get your message across'.

- After the first performance has been discussed, it is sometimes worth while to have the scene replayed by a second set of actors.

Hints

- Role playing early in a programme will help to break down inhibitions.

- Select your actors carefully.

- Where possible, allow them adequate time to improvise their 'props' and costumes.

- Encourage a light-hearted approach.

- Arrange for several role-playing sessions — try making the groups competitive.

- In multicultural groups, role acting can be a useful means of helping to break down inter-racial prejudices and promote understanding.

- Role playing is generally spontaneous, while the drama spot is usually rehearsed — there is an important area in between the two in which guidelines are established but the dialogue is spontaneous.

SEMINAR

A group whose members may each be called upon to play a formal role during its one or more study sessions, held under the guidance of a recognised authority in the subject.

Use

- To study 'in depth', under an expert.

Advantages

- Provides learning through sharing.

- An authority guides the discussion and thus promotes learning.

- A well run seminar will cover detailed and systematic discussion, thorough investigation, and careful inquiry.

Limitations

- Often the right leader is difficult to find.

- Often, too, the members are not prepared to devote the necessary amounts of time and hard work to preparing and presenting the reports.

- The expert's presence may inhibit some of the members.

- Sometimes it is difficult to research the topics and locate the sources of some of the material.

- Members will not make equal contributions — some will play only a passive role.

Requirements

- A semicircular seating arrangement is needed to promote group discussion.

- A comfortable, relaxed atmosphere is important.

- There should be facilities for note taking and for preparing reports.

- Audio-visual equipment should also be available.

Preparation and Procedure

- Define the seminar's objectives.

- Circulate the publicity material (with programme details, and background notes on the leading authority).

- The number of enrolments may have to be limited, depending on the popularity of the topic, the facilities that are available, and the wishes of the leader(s).

- A preliminary meeting should define the topic, lay down the ground rules, assign the various jobs to individuals or to working parties, and draw up reference lists.

- Reports should be presented at one or more special sessions, with any necessary visual aids available and adequate supplies of any written handouts.

- All the members should be encouraged to discuss the reports and to question the reporters.

- The seminar should be followed up by an adequate number of summarising and evaluating sessions.

Hints

- Right from the start the leader should aim at establishing a stimulating working climate and a relaxed atmosphere.

- Each member must be encouraged to participate to the fullest extent possible — involve anyone who is shy or reserved by asking them questions.

- The leader(s) should ensure that everyone who speaks keeps strictly to the topic under discussion — it is very easy to digress.

- Many topics are controversial — a balanced approach to them is desirable.

- The seminar's success will depend on thorough research, the quality of presentation, the skill of the questioners, and the extent to which each member becomes involved.

SHORT COURSES

One or more intensive-training sessions on some specific subject.

Uses

- To bring members of a group up-to-date on new developments in their field of interest.

- To provide groups of selected individuals with additional training in specific areas.

- To introduce new thinking, new insights, and new directions.

- To build morale and a sense of team spirit.

- Gets people away from their work environment to think and plan in new surroundings.

Advantages

- Can be useful in changing attitudes

- Can help to build a group into a special team.

- When attendance is voluntary, it helps to identify the persons with special interests.

- Provides great flexibility in scheduling.

- Once a clear objective has been set, the rate of progress can be geared to the various members' needs.

- Can be successful in a variety of locations.

Limitations

- People usually expect too much — the expectation rate is too high.

- Any 'conscripted' members may not respond, while 'volunteers' may not really need or profit from the training.

- The advance arrangements involve considerable work and a degree of expertise.

- The exact numbers who are to attend may not be known until the start of the course.

Requirements

- A 'cloistered' environment, away from the work site.

- A main meeting room, and a number of smaller rooms for group work.

- Such audio-visual aids as an overhead projector, paper pads, and so on.

Preparation and Procedure

- The site(s) should be set up well in advance.

- Publicity and promotion must be planned to reach the type of applicant who is likely to profit — try to find out their habits (and who their bosses are).

- Choose the course members well in advance. Provide a list of 'precourse reading' if one is needed.

- Prepare a list of 'need-to-know information' for the course members (See Chapter 4 — Managing Training.)

- Provide sessions that introduce a wide variety of training methods.

- Arrange for adequate evaluation and follow-up.

Hints

- Some reserve and uncertainty are evident whenever a group of people comes together — try to build up their confidence quietly, without embarrassing anyone.

- Prepare a precise, factual objective. (Be sure to secure the members' agreement on the course objectives before you start.)

- Start off by setting ground rules and establishing a working relationship. 'What time will we start? Can you all make it by eight o'clock? Right, eight o'clock it is — and we'll start every morning at the same time.'

- Prepare a 'map' of the accommodation and surroundings — a great deal of time can be lost in describing just where the toilets are or when the mail is likely to arrive.

- Remember to keep your programme flexible — it's what the people want to know that's important.

- Be sure that every exercise is relevant.

- Arrange some social and team-building activities — a social committee can take charge of leisure. A system of fines for 'misdemeanours' can help to amuse and provide a nucleus fund for prizes, 'rewards', and social events.

- Competing groups engender friendly rivalry and will usually enhance learning.

- Provide opportunities for group members to discover and explore any mutual interests.

SKIT

A short, rehearsed, humorous (often satirical) stage presentation involving two or more persons — can be used to gain audience response to a particular problem or situation or to promote group discussion. (Differs from role playing in that it has a prepared and rehearsed script, while role playing is impromptu).

Uses

- To introduce a topic for discussion.

- To 'highlight' a situation.

- To depict a problem.

Advantages

- Requires the active participation of at least part of the group.

- Helps to relax if it is introduced early in a training programme.

- 'Personalises' a situation and can lead to emotional involvement.

- Can 'lift' a programme by awakening a timely interest and stimulating discussion.

Limitations

- Can take considerable time and ingenuity to organise.

- Talented performers are essential.

- 'Plot' needs to be restricted to a single, clear message.

Requirements

- Should be played on a stage or against a wall (to simplify 'props').

- Must be visible to every member of the audience.

Preparation and Procedure

- Sort out your objective.

- Write the script.

- Choose the actors.

- Brief each actor.

- Assemble any necessary 'props' and costumes.

- Rehearse 'on site'.

- Brief the audience on what will be expected of them following the performance.

- The actual performance takes place.

- A discussion period follows.

- Summarise and evaluate (but only if prearranged).

Hints

- Furniture and scenery shifts should be kept to a minimum.

- Ask the actors to write their own script and to forage for any properties they may need.

- Use the skit to illustrate varying approaches to a problem ('before' and 'after' situations, for example).

- Can be used to depict class, racial, or worker-management problems.

- Can help to relieve any stresses of multiracial training. (Every group has some 'born' actors who will help to break down barriers and inhibitions).

- Look for enthusiastic actors — never force anyone into a role that could cause them embarrassment.

SYMPOSIUM

A series of short (usually five to 25 minutes) prepared speeches by up to five authorities, covering various aspects of a subject — usually followed by an audience-involvement session in which the subject is opened up.

Uses

- To present new material concisely and logically.

- To present several differing views on the one subject.

- To provide a just analysis of a controversial issue.

- To clarify conflicting aspects of a complex problem and to depict the relationships of the parts to the whole.

Advantages

- Provides for differing points of view.

- Time-limited speeches minimise digressions.

- Brief speeches help to maintain audience interest.

- A comprehensive coverage becomes possible.

- Greater resources are available to answer questions.

Limitations

- Must be run as a formal event.

- The audience does not normally participate until the final stages.

Requirements

- Every member of the audience must be able to see and hear in comfort.

- A stage and (possibly) loudspeakers may be needed for a large audience.

Procedure

- The chairman sets the scene and introduces each speaker with a few brief remarks.

- A short question period may follow each talk, or the questions may be reserved for a formal discussion period at the end.

- A period for the exchange of questions and comments between the speakers may be worthwhile, in addition to the audience's question time.

Hints

- Balance the speakers well — try to arrange an informal meeting with them beforehand, so that they get to know one another.

- The chairman needs to keep a firm control on the meeting and to see that the questions are spread evenly between the speakers — otherwise the last speaker tends to be questioned most often.

- A spread of 'arranged' questions from the audience can help to present a balanced point of view.

- Asking a guest authority to sum up finally, at the end of the discussion, is a good technique to follow.

TELECONFERENCE ('TELECON')

A preplanned telephone or satellite-link conference, involving numbers of people in various localities.

Uses

- To share information and experiences.

- To establish a working relationship, independent of distance.

Advantages

- Can save time.

- Can save money.

- More-regular meetings can be held.

- Can provide an immediate response to a developing situation.

- Can be used to explore topical issues.

- Can bring together busy experts to advise field staff and people in isolated communities.

- Improves internal communications by bringing the people in a community together for a satellite link up.

- Can establish a close working relationship by voice alone.

Limitations

- Turbulent atmospheric conditions or a faulty line will cause poor reception.

- A purely local event can prevent someone from taking part.

- People often expect too much — a teleconference is no substitute for a detailed letter or a report.

- For international calls a common language and a common technical base are needed.

Requirements

- Special arrangements must be made with your local telecommunications department.

- A quiet, disturbance-free room, with a suitable microphone or a telephone, must be available.

Preparation and Procedure

- Decide on a definite objective and a specific agenda.

- Set a precise time.

- Prepare and distribute background papers in plenty of time.

- Appoint someone to act as chairman.

- Chairman's first job must be to introduce the participants and the topic.

- The chairman calls in the participants, one at a time.

- Each speaker indicates when he/she is finished by saying 'Over to [name]'.

- The session is finished off with the 'over and out' formula.

Hints

- The more specific the topic, the more effective the conference is likely to be.

- Don't be too ambitious — keep to a simple agenda.

- Don't try to cram in too much — say rather 'I'll post you the details'.

- Speak slowly and clearly — use simple language — unless you are dealing with a team of specialists.

- Keep your messages concise and to the point.

- Check regularly on whether your message is being understood — ask leading questions, such as 'If you carry that out, what will happen?'' (*not* 'Did you understand that?')

- Make sure that each participant gets involved and has an equal share of the time.

- Plan to use your time effectively, especially on a satellite link — be considerate of the people in other countries, in different time zones.

- A number of people may be speaking before your turn comes — take notes to aid your memory and to ensure you answer any questions that are put to you.

- Make sure the telephone operator knows not to interrupt your conference call.

- A large group will confer more effectively if they use a loudspeaker-equipped telephone. Satellite terminals usually have facilities for group participation.

- Computers can be linked to transfer pictures, but the spoken word is usually more effective to explain situations and convince people.

VIDEO

An audio-visual, tape-playing (professional or amateur) device.

Uses

- To present factual material by one or more experts.

- To depict participants' responses and activities.

- To replay films.

Advantages

- Can be used to involve an audience in building its own production.

- Once purchased, it produces films relatively cheaply.

- The tapes can be used many times.

- Television programmes can be copied for showing in appropriate learning situations (but be aware of copyright restrictions).

- Ideal for showing individuals how they are performing.

Limitations

- High initial costs.

- The small screen is suitable only for small audiences (for large audiences, costly large screens are needed).

- Easy to use for rough-and-ready productions but to attain a high technical standard becomes costly.

- Large television receivers are difficult to move around.

- Can be time consuming.

Requirements

- Television set, video recorder, camera(s), tripod(s), microphone(s), and tapes.

- Sound-proof studio suitable for production and for showings.

- Camera and sound crews.

- Room in which everybody can watch the screen in comfort.

Preparation and Procedure

- Brief the 'actors'.

- Plan the objectives and the sequences.

- Write the script and practise the more difficult scenes.

- Film and edit.

- Show the finished product.

- Discuss.

- Evaluate.

Hints

- The use of video to demonstrate a skill (speaking, for example) can be time consuming — show your examples, but allow the participants to evaluate their own performance in their own time.

- People can be taught production skills in groups — get them to compete in making a short production — then invite each group in turn to introduce, demonstrate, and evaluate their effort, with an open discussion to follow each one.

- There is more to making a good film than just buying the equipment — talk to the experts before you start!

- Before you decide to buy any equipment, make sure it is compatible with what you already own.

- Do your 'homework' well before you purchase — don't listen to the glib salesman!

VISIT, FIELD TRIP, OR TOUR

Characterised by a planned itinerary, usually of a predetermined length, during which a particular environment or past or present 'event' is observed and studied.

Uses

- To relate theory to 'real' problems.

- To study something that cannot be brought into a classroom.

- To stimulate interest and concern.

- To demonstrate a course of action 'in the field' or in a work environment.

- To talk to workers in their working environment.

- To find out details of how things are done.

- To study foreign cultures or environments.

Advantages

- Seeing is more meaningful than hearing or reading alone — it becomes easier to 'relate' to the real thing.

- A particular practice can be related to its environment.

- A 'team spirit' can be fostered through participants becoming acquainted socially.

- Usually more enjoyable than classroom learning.

- Useful for competitive learning. 'Each group will prepare a report on . . . . [state topic]'.

Limitations

- Planning and organising can be time consuming.

- Travel and accommodation are costly.

- Definite numbers are often difficult to estimate.

- Tight schedules are hard to maintain.

- Certain risks are always involved — injuries or sickness, for example.

Requirements

- A definite starting time and easily identifiable starting point.

- Detailed transport, accommodation, and catering arrangements.

- Maps, information handouts, and detailed programmes for each stop.

- A final 'get together' to review the project.

Preparation and Procedure

- An organiser must plan in detail and contact every person and place that is to be visited.

- Schedules must be drawn up, and maps and handout material (or learning aids) prepared.

- Every member of the party must be well briefed on what they will see, the purpose of each visit, what will be expected of them, the amount of spare time that will be available, and the time of their return.

- After each stop, members should meet to review what they have seen and its significance for them.

Hints

- Whenever possible, someone should make a preliminary tour to check on the details and the timing.

- If a preliminary tour is not possible, check the schedules and preliminary plans and resolve any difficulties well beforehand by telephone, later confirming in writing whatever is agreed upon.

- Build in social activities to provide for recreation.

- No schedule should be too 'tight' — always try to allow for the unexpected or the unpredictable.

- Make sure that each of the contact points is known by everybody who needs to know it.

- Don't take anything for granted — telephone ahead each night, to ensure that the arrangements still stand.

- The project can be made more meaningful by asking for a detailed report on it afterward — either individually or competitively, in groups.

- All members must be told what will be required of them before they set out.

WORKSHOP

Usually, a group that is 'in retreat' from a common workplace or similar workplaces in order to share work-related common interests; to improve individual work performances; to extend knowledge through intensive study, research, and discussion; or to solve their work-related problems by sharing common experiences and knowledge.

Uses

- To identify, explore, and seek solutions to work-related problems.

- For in-depth study of a situation (background and social and philosophical implications).

- To plan for future activities.

- To build up a text or construct proceedings (trainer's manual, for example).

- To develop a working philosophy.

- As part of a convention or conference to study brief, related topics or problems.

Advantages

- Can assemble and take advantage of a great deal of experience.

- Designed for a high degree of participation.

- Allows for group-determined goals, plans, and recommendations.

- Competition between 'rival' groups is possible.

- A well run workshop maintains the interest and enthusiasm of its members.

- It will generate more ideas than any individual would produce alone, and will promote confidence in agreed-upon solutions.

Limitations

- Its organisation and running are time consuming.

- Requires a high staff-to-student ratio.

- Requires more space and equipment than normally needed for a lecture series.

- Its members must be willing and able to work independently and yet to co-operate closely.

Requirements

- A common meeting place, with additional rooms for workshops.

- Seats should be arranged in a semicircle (avoid theatre-type seating).

- An adequate library and other resource materials are required for research.

- Audio-visual materials for recording ideas and reporting back to full groups (large paper pads or overlays are ideal for this — with the help of 'blue-tack' or masking tape, you can paper a wall with the sheets and thus build up a complete story or compare a series of reports).

Preparation and Procedure

- Set clear objectives and goals.

- Planning — How big? When? Where? How long (half day, five weeks)?

- Should 'proceedings' be recorded and published — Who would do the work? How and when would it be done?

- Try to ensure the members are selected for their potential contribution and their experience rather than for reasons of prestige or seniority.

- Check on the physical facilities and material requirements well in advance.

- Arrange for an adequate number of carefully chosen resource persons to be on hand.

- Draft the detailed timetable.

- Prepare the 'need-to-know' information handout (for a residential workshop this should include the travel arrangements, details of the sleeping accommodation, the mail collection and delivery times, meal times, the whereabouts of the toilets, and similar details). See Chapter 4—Managing Training.

- Make sure someone is on hand to welcome each new arrival, to help anyone with problems, and to answer any queries that may arise.

- Follow up the workshop with a final evaluating and 'strengths and weaknesses' session.

Hints

- Start with discussion in pairs, but get group discussions going as soon as possible.

- Printed workshop proceedings are worth the effort it takes to produce them — they reinforce the learning and will later provide a useful reference source.

- 'Democratic discipline' should govern all the workshop activities— draw up a 'working contract' that sets out all necessary details — 'What time shall we start?', Shall we set up a social committee?', and so on.

- Although any programme needs to be flexible, its timing must be carefully planned. (Allow for 'reporting back'.) If there isn't enough time for every group's report, ask the non-reporting groups for any ideas that have not already been covered—but remember that a strict time schedule is essential to enable as many groups as possible to participate. Appoint a timekeeper to sound a warning bell (striking a spoon against a cup will do if no bell is available) a minute or so before time is up, and another 'bell' at full time.

- It often proves a good idea to invite the opening speaker to stress the importance of the workshop (select speaker and topic to provide a fresh perspective on members' work and responsibilities).

- Precise workshop goals and objectives should be approved and adopted on the first day.

- Foster competitiveness in setting up a group-reporting system—but make sure it is light hearted rather than serious.

"Little of what we passively listen to is remembered. The greater our involvement the more we learn."

116

FURTHER READING FROM KOGAN PAGE

The Mager Library

Analysing Performance Problems Robert F Mager and Peter Pipe

Developing Attitude Toward Learning Robert F Mager

Goal Analysis Robert F Mager

Making Instruction Work Robert F Mager

Measuring Instructional Results (second edn) Robert F Mager

Preparing Instructional Objectives Robert F Mager

The Practical Trainer Series

How to Design and Deliver Induction Training Programmes Michael Meighan

How to Take a Training Audit Michael Applegarth

A Practical Approach to Group Training David Leigh